TO

FROM

DATE

40 Days of Hope
for Healthcare Heroes

40 DAYS OF

HOPE

FOR HEALTHCARE

HEROES

AMY K. SORRELLS, BSN, RN

Tyndale House Publishers
Carol Stream, Illinois

**LIVING
EXPRESSIONS**
COLLECTION

Living Expressions invites you to explore God's
Word in a way that is refreshing to the spirit
and restorative to the soul.

Visit Tyndale online at tyndale.com.

Visit Amy K. Sorrells at amyksorrells.com.

TYNDALE, Tyndale's quill logo, *Living Expressions*, and the Living Expressions logo are
registered trademarks of Tyndale House Ministries.

40 Days of Hope for Healthcare Heroes

Edited by Kathryn S. Olson

Designed by Jacqueline L. Nuñez

Published in association with the literary agency of WordServe Literary, wordserveliterary.com.

Scripture quotations are taken from the *Holy Bible*, New Living Translation, copyright ©
1996, 2004, 2015 by Tyndale House Foundation. Used by permission of Tyndale House
Publishers, Carol Stream, Illinois 60188. All rights reserved.

While the stories in *40 Days of Hope for Healthcare Heroes* are inspired by real-life experiences,
all names, events, establishments, organizations, and locales have been changed to protect
the privacy of both healthcare workers and their patients. Any resemblance to actual
persons, living or dead, businesses, companies, or events is entirely coincidental.

For information about special discounts for bulk purchases, please contact Tyndale House
Publishers at csresponse@tyndale.com, or call 1-855-277-9400.

ISBN 978-1-4964-5587-1

Printed in the United States of America

27	26	25	24	23	22	21
7	6	5	4	3	2	1

To Birdie Gunyon Meyer, RN, MA, PMH-C,
who not only saved my life,
but also convinced me to enter that one little contest

and

In loving memory of
Jimmy Wayne "Jim" Hendrich
February 2, 1950–April 8, 2018
Police officer and tireless advocate of healthcare and first responder heroes

Dear Reader.

This is not a normal devotional. Nothing about being in healthcare now—or even before the pandemic—was really normal, after all. Our irreverent laughter veils the ache in our hearts, a sign of moral injury resulting from a stressed healthcare system. We wear watches that remind us to "breathe." Behind our masks, fear and exhaustion plague us. Face shields can't protect us from the ambivalence we feel at work when we put our patients first, and know at the same time we are risking the health of our family and friends. This devotional is an attempt to gather the most common challenges and laments, joy, laughter, and hope we face at work to re-center us to our calling.

To some, the anecdotes may seem a bit jarring—and in truth, some of them are. But as healthcare workers in the middle of the battle for patient-centered care while pressured to raise satisfaction scores, reverence is often the last thing on our minds. Out of the patients' view, we are raw. We are ineloquent. We are abrupt and elbow deep in the mania of patient lives, while trying to cope with the demands and safety of our families. Appropriate coping is often an enigma for those of us who spend the majority of our days on the front lines. And yet, if we don't find ways to take care of our hearts, we won't be able to take care of our patients. If we don't find ways to turn our faces toward the Lord in the midst of the pain of our work, we will spiral into despair, as so many of our colleagues already have.

That's what this book is about.

A couple of caveats: Most of these chapters are not my own personal experiences. Just like the teamwork exhibited in hospitals every day, multiple healthcare workers from across the country and across varied disciplines contributed thoughts, snippets of stories, essays, and even tears. To respect patient privacy, the utmost care has been taken to change names as well as to combine and/or rearrange scenarios and patient outcomes. I also took the liberty of writing each story in first person, in order to give you intimate access to the real-life emotion of each story.

It is my prayer that by the end of this book, you as a healthcare professional will know it's okay to not be okay. We are trained to be strong and stoic, but now more than ever we need permission to admit we cannot do it all, at work or at home. It's okay to be angry and fearful about pandemics and epidemics and overtime and overload. It's okay if you don't feel God's presence, you don't see him, and you don't agree with him. It's okay to not want to go on, to feel frustrated and exhausted and spent. It's okay to talk to God about all that. He is quite big enough to handle it.

Believe it or not, the Lord covets our complaints and pleas, even as we covet our next day off.

Most of all, it is my prayer that through these words you will rediscover your purpose and calling as a healer and a hero.

God chose you, after all.

And the world needs you now more than ever.

Amy K. Sorrells

DAY 1

For you are all one in Christ Jesus.

GALATIANS 3:28

"**H**e's out of his mind," my night-shift colleague said as she gave me a report on the patient in room 474. "He's talking nonsense. Wrist restraints and hand mitts on. He fell off a curb and fractured his left lower leg; an ambulance brought him here. But he can't tell us about, and we can't locate, any family."

The situation wasn't unusual in our big-city hospital, where drifters, drug addicts, and dementia patients brought in from nursing homes often lacked family or other support. When I entered the man's room, I expected to perform the usual assessment and to do my best to keep him clean and comfortable. But as soon as I saw him, I knew something was amiss.

Mr. Sobol beckoned me closer to his bed, reaching for me with both hands, even though they were held in place with restraints. I came closer, keeping distant enough so that if he was suffering from delusional dementia, I would be clear of the punches and pinching I'd learned the hard way to avoid. But rather than becoming more agitated as I approached, his countenance softened, if only slightly.

He spoke to me with urgency, but the sounds he made were unrecognizable.

"I'm Beth, your nurse. I'm here to help you. Do you understand?"

He repeated the same sounds, his grip on my hand tight with desperation. We both wanted to understand each other. But we couldn't.

Soon, though, I began to recognize the repeating consonants and vowels that indicated he likely was speaking another language, and not what coworkers had been calling gibberish.

Eventually, his locution slowed and the near-panic in his eyes receded. I eventually determined he was from Belarus. The hospital operator helped secure an interpreter who spoke Russian on a three-way line.

"*Privyet*, Joseph!" the translator said.

Joseph's eyes brightened instantly when he realized he had a connection, a way to communicate, a way to finally be understood.

Over the course of the next few days, we scheduled meetings with Russian-speaking interpreters and each of Joseph's physicians. We learned he had a sister in Chicago with whom he could stay once healthy enough to discharge. He had been traveling to see her on a Greyhound bus, and when he'd gotten off at the Indianapolis station to stretch his legs and use the restroom, he'd fallen. Unfamiliar with his language or accent, people at the bus station assumed he was drunk, and the misunderstanding continued from there.

Two days later, Joseph was sitting in a chair beside his bed, his leg propped on a pillow and a stool, his sister Tetiana sitting beside him, ready to take him home.

BREAKROOM BOOST

Language isn't the only barrier that keeps us from giving the best care. The more stressed we are, the more detached we become from our work, and the fewer reserves we have to dig deeper to understand our patients' point of view. But God is so much greater than our weakness and the darkness that revels in division. Compassion is greater than confusion. Encouragement is greater than exhaustion. Peace is greater than powerlessness. In Christ, we are more than conquerors of the irritability and weariness that threaten the caregiving we so want to offer.

HANDWASHING PRAYER

Lord, help me to listen for you and to hear with my heart when I'm tempted to dismiss things I don't understand.

Record today's fears, frustrations, and heartbreak:

_____

_____

_____

_____

_____

EVIDENCE-BASED HOPE

Record things you are grateful for and where you've seen God working
this week:

_____

_____

_____

_____

_____

DAY 2

Love each other. Just as I have loved you,
you should love each other.
JOHN 13:34

It was a year to remember: 1995—the year of *Braveheart*, blue M&M's, the Oklahoma City bombing, Mariah Carey, and the Atlanta Braves. It was also the summer I watched, helpless, as a young gay man died alone of AIDS at age twenty-six.

Only two years younger than he was and fresh out of nursing school, I peered into Greg's isolation room from the hall. Like many patients, Greg was alone in his room most of the day except when we came in to check his vital signs every four hours. With his hair mostly gone and his bones at harsh angles beneath the sheets, he lay on his side watching the traffic on the interstate outside his window.

I donned the yellow impermeable gown and pulled gloves on my hands, then put on the mask and face shield, all required at the time, despite the work of Ryan White and others to dispel the myths about transmission.

"How are you today, Greg?"

He did not reply, but kept staring out the window. I couldn't blame him for being depressed. Not only was he dying, but he wasn't allowed to see his partner, Brian, either.

I'd been in the room setting up his IV medications the week before, when he'd begged his parents to let Brian visit. I saw his mother wince and his father leave the room. Their decision was final, and in 1995 Greg and Brian didn't have any rights.

Since then, Greg hadn't spoken to anyone. As his primary nurse, I felt so helpless. What could I possibly do for him?

The idea came to me as I spread a new sheet and blanket over his legs. I rummaged around in the supply and linen rooms until I'd gathered everything I needed.

Back in the room, I filled a basin with soapy warm water, tossed in several washrags, and carried it to his bedside table. I gently lifted his

9

legs, the skin a patchwork of purple and red Kaposi's sarcoma lesions, and spread towels and impervious pads underneath them.

I pulled a stool up to the end of the bed. "Is it okay if I wash your feet?"

Greg looked away from the interstate and focused on me. The incredulity and gratitude in his eyes nearly rendered me too emotional to continue with what I'd set out to do for him. But wash his feet I did. With each washcloth, I wondered how long it had been since he had felt touch. I wondered when his parents stopped hugging him. I wondered how it felt to be a contemporary leper.

After his feet were washed, I gently massaged lotion into them, between his toes, around his ankles, and over his lower legs. By the time I finished, he had closed his eyes and fallen asleep. The hard, empty stare was replaced by a countenance relaxed and at peace.

And I knew I was not helpless after all.

BREAKROOM BOOST

As healthcare workers, we encounter the untouchable, unthinkable, and unimaginable every day. It's so hard to know how to assuage the wounds of the heart that the deftest and most daring of surgeons could never reach. When all we have to give a patient is love, we can give it. When the chasm of loneliness appears too gaping to cross, we can use love to bridge it. When we are rushed and weary, we can draw on the peace and strength that passes understanding.

HANDWASHING PRAYER

Lord, friend and healer of lepers, help me to be the love my most marginalized patient needs. There's so much anger and hatred in the world. Help me remember above all to love others, just as you have loved all the leper-like parts of me.

Record today's fears, frustrations, and heartbreak:

_____

_____

_____

_____

EVIDENCE-BASED HOPE

Record things you are grateful for and where you've seen God working this week:

_____

_____

_____

_____

DAY 3

He holds all creation together.
COLOSSIANS 1:17

"I'm going to need some help in here," called Mike, the emergency department triage nurse, as he and the patient's wife guided the weak and shaky man to one of the trauma rooms.

As an emergency room physician, I was well-accustomed to assessing the urgency of a situation in seconds. In this case, the look on Mike's face was the first indication that this was not a good situation. The splats of blood trailing behind them on the floor were the second.

I was familiar with Mr. Jackson from other times he had come in for complications from his tracheostomy and rapidly progressing laryngeal cancer. That he was bleeding again, and significantly, made me catch my breath with dread.

Sarah, another nurse, hooked up the suction as we guided Mr. Jackson to the gurney. Bright red blood splattered the sides of the suction container on the wall, and quickly collected in the bottom.

Mr. Jackson's eyes darted wildly between his wife and the nurses and paused when he saw me come to his side. I felt eyes of the team members on me as they scurried to set up a second suction, sponges, and more.

"Mr. Jackson, we're going to do everything we can to take good care of you, to keep you comfortable." I did my best to assure him. I prayed he would not sense my lack of assurance and peace.

He blinked and nodded, even as I could see the suction container already almost filled with 250 cc of blood and rising rapidly.

"Mike, see who's on call for head and neck. Have Lucy call and see if we can get a transfer downtown, if they can get an OR ready," I directed. But I had a sinking feeling there would not be time for either a transfer or surgery.

Sarah, two more nurses, and a respiratory therapist worked on inserting intravenous lines, setting up a rapid blood infuser, and other resuscitative devices. The house supervisor and social worker guided the pale and near-hysterical wife to a quiet room down the hall, away from the ghastly scene.

Within minutes, our goal of fixing the bleeding switched to keeping Mr. Jackson as comfortable as we could.

This was not going to end well.

Mr. Jackson's previous scans showed the tumor wrapped around his carotid artery, a dreadful but not unexpected end-stage neck cancer progression. The problem was, no one—neither his surgeon nor his oncologist—had prepared the patient for this. No one had prepared his wife. And not even the most stoic, seasoned team of caregivers can prepare themselves, let alone a patient, for bleeding to death.

Within the hour, Mr. Jackson succumbed. Afterwards, I spent over an hour with his wife, explaining what had happened and why we could not save him. By the time I returned to my station, I was a dozen patients behind, and I had a completely traumatized staff to lead as well.

As the next shift arrived, I gathered the team members who had worked on Mr. Jackson in an empty procedure room. As inadequate as I felt in that moment to provide encouragement, I knew if we didn't process what had happened before we went home, we could all carry it with us and it would emerge, like so many unprocessed traumas, as anger or burnout or any other countless unhealthy coping mechanisms.

"First of all, that was awful."

Two of the nurses wiped silent tears, permission finally freeing them.

"Let's talk about it."

We dialogued for over an hour, weeping together, venting about the injustice and unfairness of the situation, lamenting our inability to save him, embracing, acknowledging each other, affirming that we—each of us—had done all we could.

BREAKROOM BOOST

In this desperate situation, the medical staff did all they could, just as you have done in similar scenarios. They comforted Mr. Jackson. They comforted his wife. The work of their minds and the passion of their hearts and the touch of their hands filled this patient up even as his life blood ran dry. In this world we will have trouble and undeserved disease and death. But take heart, Jesus has overcome all this and more.

HANDWASHING PRAYER

Remind me that in times of trouble, my heart is yours, Lord. Thank you for being my help.

VITAL SIGNS

Record today's fears, frustrations, and heartbreak:

_____

_____

_____

_____

_____

EVIDENCE-BASED HOPE

Record things you are grateful for and where you've seen God working this week:

_____

_____

_____

_____

_____

DAY 4

I am alone and in deep distress.
My problems go from bad to worse.
PSALM 25:16-17

I stare at the blinking light on the desk phone and eye the unit secretary across the nurses' station. She eyes me back apologetically. It's room 103's wife. Again. The fourth time today, and it's only 11:00.

Doesn't she know I have four other patients, three of them in isolation, one who will need to be transferred to the progressive care unit, one complaining about not getting their bed bath, a half dozen new stat orders from the rounding physicians, and my blood sugar machine just shut down and won't work again until I run a quality control test on it? Why does she think she and her husband are the only ones I have to take care of today?

I shut my eyes and try to take a moment, a breath, to reorient my heart, to settle my frayed nerves, to keep myself from counting the minutes until my lunch break. I try to think of the man in room 103, about his test results that gleamed bold and bright red and all wrong on the computer screen that morning, too high and too low numbers that screamed the dire condition of his weakening body. I think of the way he grinned as best he could when the aide and I shaved his jowls and trimmed his overgrown eyebrows and combed the hair he had left across his near-bald head. I think of the dribble of milk I wiped off his chin as he tried and failed to neatly spoon cereal into his mouth with his jittering, age-spotted hands.

I try to think of his wife behind the blinking hold light on the phone. Maybe she's sitting by their kitchen window, watching the birds pecking at the empty feeders he built so long ago and was in charge of keeping filled. Maybe she's sitting on the bed they've shared, the mattress now sagging in the middle where they have spooned for decades.

I try to imagine so I don't lose my temper when she asks me the same set of questions about what doctors have seen him and what the doctors have said and what the doctors intend to do for the fourth time in as many hours.

I have no new answers for her.

Nothing has changed with her husband. Not his vital signs. Not his mental status. Not the fact that he was just diagnosed with colon cancer. And not the fact that she can't visit her groom of fifty-seven years, no exceptions, because of the COVID-19 pandemic.

Help me, Jesus, I pray silently.

At first the words are in vain.

But then I realize I really do need his help.

I pick up the receiver. I take a moment to rehearse words in my head, so they sound calm and kind. And I press the button next to the flashing light. "How can I help you?" I ask.

And I mean it.

BREAKROOM BOOST

Patients and families are frustrating. But behind their never-ending questions and complaints is often fear. In the midst of short staffing and the minute-by-minute triaging of your day, when you feel your nerves fraying, turn your heart to Jesus. Before we even ask, he knows our needs and pleas. He sees the patients, too, and he will give us peace and the ability to care. He never expected us to do all things— that's his job. Only he can do everything. He can give us the strength to work for him.

HANDWASHING PRAYER

Show me the way, Lord, when I am too tired and forget to ask you for help. Show me how to care when I don't feel like I have any caring left to give.

Record today's fears, frustrations, and heartbreak:

_____

_____

_____

_____

EVIDENCE-BASED HOPE

Record things you are grateful for and where you've seen God working
this week:

_____

_____

_____

_____

DAY 5

Don't look out only for your own interests,
but take an interest in others, too.

PHILIPPIANS 2:4

The cadence of cicadas filled the summer night air as my partner and I walked through the automatic double doors of the emergency department. Bombarded by medical and psychosocial emergencies on several units from the time we'd arrived at the hospital for our security shift that afternoon—two code blues, a shoplifter in the hospital gift shop, a domestic disturbance on the postpartum unit, a desperate drug-seeker in the emergency department, and more—we welcomed the chance to be outside.

But the reprieve was short-lived.

The reason for our summons to the emergency department sat before us, a white Lexus parked haphazardly in the roundabout. The passenger side door hung open, hinting at the chaos that had ensued moments prior. Blood- and fluid-soaked seats and floorboards, and an oversized, pink, quilted diaper bag left behind indicated the hurried events. As hospital officers, we are accustomed to the unexpected, but every so often a case like this one surprises us.

Giving birth in the car had not been in this mother's birthing plan, but neither nature nor the baby girl cared to comply this evening. In the flurry of the birth and getting mother and baby to the postpartum unit, the father had left the keys dangling in the ignition.

My partner and I looked at each other, knowing we couldn't just park the soiled car in the parking lot. Neither was it likely that the father would notice it was missing.

"Let's take it down to the dock," I suggested.

So, with the image of the valet stealing Cameron's dad's 1961 Ferrari 250 GT in *Ferris Bueller's Day Off* not far from our minds, we drove the Lexus around the hospital to the back docks where supplies came and waste went, and parked the soiled vehicle as close as we could to one of the empty bays.

We gathered all the cleaning supplies we could find, took the seats completely out of the car, and scrubbed and wiped and vacuumed and detailed that car to better-than-new.

As the sun rose on that new day, my partner and I stood together and marveled with a little bit of pride at the work we had done, knowing that if our own wives had delivered—let alone in our cars—how much a detailing would mean to us in that moment.

I took the keys to the father, who was at his wife's side on the postpartum unit.

"Good as new," I said with a wink, tossing him the keys.

Later, the father sent a letter to the hospital's CEO, commending Juan and me for our efforts.

But the letter didn't mean near as much as the look on that father's face as he sat on the bed next to his glowing wife, holding their brand-new baby girl.

BREAKROOM BOOST
The upholstery of a car might seem insignificant in the grand scheme of chaos in the world. But God is in the small and the big things. He is in the births and the deaths, the joy and the mourning, and in the big picture and the details—and detailing—of life.

HANDWASHING PRAYER
Lord, help me see you in the small things I do every day, as well as the big things. Thank you that you are in all of it.

VITAL SIGNS
Record today's fears, frustrations, and heartbreak:

_____

_____

_____

_____

Record things you are grateful for and where you've seen God working this week:

_____

_____

_____

_____

_____

_____

_____

_____

_____

DAY 6

Everything is meaningless—like chasing the wind.

ECCLESIASTES 2:17

Saturday is bath day on the neonatal intensive care unit, a reprieve from the tubes and monitors, miniature formula measurements and charting. I marvel as much as my premature patients at the warm, silky feel of water against fragile skin, the soothing scent of lavender baby bath soap, the wide-eyed pleasure of limbs gently massaged and tiny bodies snuggly swaddled.

Some babies have mamas and daddies who thoughtfully choose and set out sweet, freshly laundered onesies with matching blankets and crib sheets for us to use on bath days.

Others, like baby Jack, don't have many visitors, and so I head to the supply room to choose for him. Rummaging through donation bins arranged by sex and size, I find a pale blue onesie with an embroidered puppy dog on the chest, a pale blue and white striped crib sheet, and a standard hospital-issue newborn blanket for swaddling.

I can hear Jack screaming from across the unit when I open the supply room door, and I am not surprised. I will be holding him for most of the shift, when my other babies are settled, because settling is not something sweet Jack can do. Not with the help of the electric swing. Not with the help of volunteers who come to rock babies. Not with the help of the morphine and methadone and other medication I titrate to help ease his withdrawal from the merciless opioid addiction he battles.

For seven weeks now, we've taken turns holding Jack as he shakes, bouncing him on our hips when he wails, watching in vain as he tries to breathe through sneezing fits and his sweet, stuffed-up button nose, and encouraging him as he fights and spits out the nipple when we try to feed him.

We watch every Friday afternoon as the social worker escorts his mother to his room at the end of the hall, and we pretend not to judge the young girl with the scarred arms and hollow eyes, the young girl battling her own addiction and withdrawal. We pretend not to hope that she will fail to meet the prerequisites that would allow her to take Jack home. We pretend not to care as much as we do for the red-faced, inconsolable baby boy with the puppy-dog onesie and pale blue blanket who will discharge in his mother's arms and die three weeks later, in spite of all we did to try to save him.

Dear God, was I, were we, just prolonging Jack's suffering in his short time on earth? Could he even feel our care, a poor substitute for a real mom's love, through the haze of medication we had to give him?

Did it even matter that I bothered to match his onesie with his crib sheet on bath days?

BREAKROOM BOOST

The Lord knew Jack before he was formed. God sculpted his sweet fingers and toes. God was with him in the secret spaces of his mother's womb. Jack was fearfully and wonderfully made, and the choices of his mother have no authority over the days God ordained for him to be here on earth. If only for a short while, Jack knew arms that held him tight because of one of us. Jack knew soft kisses on his forehead because of one of us. Jack knew the scent of lavender baby soap and freshly washed sheets. He knew the feel of a breast against his face, the pat of a hand against his back, the sound of a lullaby in the wee hours of the morning. Jack knew these things because of one of us, and because the Lord knew we could provide them.

HANDWASHING PRAYER

Lord, life is so short for some. Help me see you in every moment. Help me be the touch someone like Jack so desperately needs.

Record today's fears, frustrations, and heartbreak:

_____

_____

_____

_____

EVIDENCE-BASED HOPE

Record things you are grateful for and where you've seen God working this week:

_____

_____

_____

_____

DAY 7

Don't copy the behavior and customs of this world.

ROMANS 12:2

I tiptoed around the cage crib where the two-year-old girl lay motionless, limbs propped and cushioned on blanket rolls, her tender face illuminated by the light of a half dozen IV pumps. As her primary nurse this shift in the pediatric intensive care unit, I was constantly titrating her medications in an endeavor to keep her sedated, dull her pain, paralyze her so she didn't fight against the work of the ventilator, and at the same time keep her blood pressure from declining.

At the foot of Rachel's steel-barred bed lay a threadbare rag doll, dressed in a plain blue dress and wearing a bonnet resembling the one her grandmother wore when she wasn't sleeping on the sleeper sofa next to Rachel's bed, as she was now. Surveying all the tubes and wires and monitors and pumps, I realized this was likely more technology than this Amish family had ever encountered.

They'd been making soap, several mothers and grandmothers together, Lavina said. Little Rachel followed the older children around the farm, tended to by her older siblings, but she'd slipped off to find her mother. Enthralled with a bucket of lye, she'd dipped her dimpled hand in and eaten it before anyone noticed. She was airlifted in from the remote hospital closest to her community, but the lye severely burned clear through her throat and esophagus, leading to the deadly sepsis smoldering in her bloodstream.

Void of management and the commotion of daytime, night shift lends itself to deeper conversations with parents and grandparents who stay with children during their admissions. As Lavina stayed with Rachel at night to give her parents a much-needed break, she and I shared some very special quiet nighttime chats. I wondered if she struggled as I did to reconcile the complicated, computerized aspects of Rachel's care with the little I knew about her faith, known for devotion to simplicity.

"How do you reconcile all the technology with your faith?" I asked her one night as the ventilator whooshed and whirred, keeping Rachel's little body oxygenated. I felt like God gave me my brain to learn the science to care for sick children. Did Lavina feel the same way about God's calling on her life?

"Just because we don't use machines and technology ourselves does not mean that we don't feel like God gave others the ability. We are so grateful for the skills of the doctors and nurses."

"What about when our technology fails?"

Lavina studied me for a moment, her face crinkling into a soft, sympathetic looking smile. She reached out and enveloped Rachel's limp hand in hers, veiny and calloused. "Young, old, we are like a vapor, like dust. God's will shall be done. Even if it means letting Rachel go."

Within a few days, God called Rachel home. She was in heaven, I felt certain.

Weeks later, a simple letter arrived addressed to me from Lavina. Several pages long, it explained more about their way of life and her eighth grade education, her grief and her faith. I keep that letter tucked into the twelfth chapter of the book of Romans, to remind me that the line between faith and skills is often blurred, and neither can fully separate from the other.

BREAKROOM BOOST

Healing was at the top of Jesus' to-do list throughout his ministry. But healing isn't always possible in the physical sense, as we know all too well. What feels like personal failure is not only emotionally but also morally exhausting. The pain of relinquishing time allocated to a soul on earth to God is only assuaged by reminding ourselves that our integrity and diligent pursuit of best practice is the best gift we can give to a patient transitioning to eternity—and their family. God's will be done, indeed.

HANDWASHING PRAYER

Lord, help me see beyond the technology of medicine to the heart of the patient and family, and to rest in your greater, ineffable plans.

VITAL SIGNS

Record today's fears, frustrations, and heartbreak:

_____

_____

_____

_____

_____

_____

EVIDENCE-BASED HOPE

Record things you are grateful for and where you've seen God working this week:

_____

_____

_____

_____

_____

_____

DAY 8

My help comes from the LORD,
who made heaven and earth!
PSALM 121:2

"**B**onnie Miller?" I called into the nearly full waiting room of the cardiology clinic.

A droopy-shouldered, white-haired woman stood, one shaky hand holding tight to a cane, and the other pulling an oxygen tank behind her. A slightly less hunched, gray-haired man stood, and the two of them began a painstakingly slow shuffle toward me. My stomach growled, and I felt the irritability that meant it was well past lunchtime for me and my fellow nursing assistants, and we had three more patients to see. I figured the pair were husband and wife, but a second look indicated otherwise. She looked too old to be his wife. His shirt was buttoned to the neck, making him appear schoolboyish though he had to be at least in his sixties.

Could this be a mother and son?

I glanced at Bonnie's chart again. She was eighty-one. It was quite possible.

"This way," I said, holding the door open for them to the clinic rooms.

Ms. Miller guided her son, who stood at least a foot taller than her, to follow me. Soon it became evident that he was nonverbal.

I ushered the two of them into a room and took a set of vital signs on Bonnie as I tried to learn a little more about them. Widowed for fifteen years, she was the full-time caregiver for Ernie, her sixty-seven-year-old developmentally delayed son. Two other sons lived on opposite coasts and had families of their own; it had been some time since she had seen or heard from them.

"We never could stand the thought of putting him in a home," she said, patting his hand.

He seemed not to notice, appearing intrigued with the photograph on the opposite wall.

I didn't blame her. But as I went through her medication list and made note of her blue-tinged fingernails and edematous ankles, I realized she was, as her chart indicated, in the last stages of heart failure.

What would happen to Ernie when she died?

How did she manage to care for him even now?

"Ms. Miller," I started.

She held her hand up. "I know what you're thinking. People look at this old bag of bones all the time and ask what I expect to happen to him." Her eyes softened with emotion. "My husband and I made plans a long time ago, right before he died. There's a small nursing home down the road where Ernie has a spot all paid for if he needs it."

She glanced at him in a way reminiscent of a young mother doting on a child.

"I've been taking care of him myself for all these years. I'm not about to abandon him just because God calls me to heaven."

She taught me more about love and devotion in that short visit than most people do in a lifetime.

BREAKROOM BOOST

From young King David to Jesus, Scripture reminds us that outward appearances can belie a person's heart, calling, and intentions. A scrawny adolescent killed a giant. A crazy old man built an ark. A murderer was given the Ten Commandments. Sarah had a baby despite being well advanced in age. In a world hyper-focused on appearance, we can't help the snap judgments that come to mind during our busy days. At the start of your days, pray for the belt of truth, for feet that bring peace, and for diligence and awareness of opportunities to see beyond circumstance and demeanor.

HANDWASHING PRAYER

Lord, when I'm tempted to rush to judgment, help me remember that you alone know a person's heart.

Record today's fears, frustrations, and heartbreak:

_____

_____

_____

_____

EVIDENCE-BASED HOPE

Record things you are grateful for and where you've seen God working this week:

_____

_____

_____

_____

DAY 9

A cry is heard in Ramah . . .

JEREMIAH 31:15

I swept the blond, sweat-dampened hair from the forehead of the boy named Samuel, and my breath caught in my throat. A distinct line divided his sunburned, freckled brow from the pale skin over which his home haircut had fallen, evidence of hours spent working livestock and chasing grasshoppers across the patchwork fields of his rural Indiana home.

Samuel's grandfather had found him collapsed among shoulder-high corn rows, unconscious for who knows how long. The boy had been well, albeit tired, at breakfast, his mother reported, her eyes searching ours for answers, hope, salvation we did not possess.

Diabetic ketoacidosis, DKA, was the diagnosis at the top of Samuel's care plan. Sneaky and silent in children, the disease is often caused by viruses that settle in and attack the pancreas without any outward sign. Subtle indications like fatigue and excess thirst and frequent urination can easily be explained by the hard play—or work, in Samuel's case—of a farm boy's life. Once a patient with DKA reaches the pediatric intensive care unit, our ability to combat the advanced mayhem is precarious as we struggle against an unpredictable balance between lowering extraordinarily high blood sugars and protecting the brain.

I adjusted the rate of the insulin dripping into his veins in an attempt to save the wide-eyed dreams and play of this innocent boy. But in the end, the cerebral edema proved inevitable, the chemical processes beyond our human influence proved too enigmatic, and we were left with the chore of helping him die peacefully as his brain herniated literally before our eyes.

Tests were performed to confirm brain death.

The chaplain, the social worker, and the organ procurement team were called.

And as we worked through the night to keep his physical body working for the sake of organ recipients and family farewells, I imagined

Samuel's soul flying free over the fields he had roamed. I wondered if the angels ushering him to heaven would hear his mother's sobs. I wondered if I'd ever get over the sunburn so fresh on Samuel's freckled brow.

BREAKROOM BOOST
God heard the cries, as he heard those in Ramah. He collected every tear. And he wishes the world had never gone so wrong that anyone, especially a child, dies. But God was with Samuel every second, in the leap of those grasshoppers, and in the laughter of him and his friends as they played under the brilliant blue sky, heads bobbing amidst the rows of beans. In the darkness of that pediatric intensive care room, your touch and your love ushered him into the arms of the Lord. No, it's not fair. It's not right. But you should see him now, running fast and free. And you should hear him, laughing, as he runs into the arms of God.

HANDWASHING PRAYER
Lord, I don't understand your ways. But thank you that there is heaven for patients like Samuel and for all of us.

VITAL SIGNS
Record today's fears, frustrations, and heartbreak:

_____

_____

_____

_____

_____

_____

Record things you are grateful for and where you've seen God working this week:

_____

_____

_____

_____

_____

_____

DAY 10

It is the smallest of all seeds, but it becomes the largest of garden plants; it grows into a tree, and birds come and make nests in its branches.
MATTHEW 13:32

"What's up, rookie?" The charge nurse, Sue, grinned.

She loved to tease me about being the youngest person in the pharmacy department. For my first job right out of school, I'd been desperate for the drama of an emergency department or big-city trauma ward. Instead, I was assigned to the hospice unit, the absolute last on my list of career goals. Surely I'd gone to school for more than titrating pain and nausea medication dosages.

"Living the dream," I replied, stuffing my lunch bag into the over-filled staff refrigerator.

"Peanut butter and jelly again?" she asked.

"Peanut butter and jelly. Again." I was also a newlywed living five hundred miles away from family and friends, and my husband and I were on a tight budget, saving all we could to buy a house.

Sue always arrived for her shift with a smile on her face and a sparkle in her eyes. About ten years older than me, she was married and raising small children. Often I wondered how she cared for little ones at home and worked full time with patients who were dying. Didn't that take a toll on her emotions and physical being? Wouldn't she rather be working in the emergency department or as a school nurse or anything more uplifting than this? Yet Sue had a peace and beauty about her that seemed almost angelic.

One day after a particularly difficult morning update, Sue and I were alone in the breakroom. I asked her how she worked day in and day out with patients who were dying—some who had great faith and others who were afraid to close their eyes, fearing they wouldn't wake again.

"It's an honor and privilege to care for others in their last days on this earth," she said with that beautiful smile, explaining that she felt she was preparing them for their final journey, and that she tried in some small way to bring comfort to them and their families.

Despite my lack of enthusiasm about hospice, the pharmacy and unit staff became my family, encouraging me and bolstering my professional—and personal—confidence. Eventually, I became the lead pharmacist for the hospice unit. I attended morning rounds, receiving patient updates, providing patient medication recommendations to physicians and nursing staff, and meeting with family members and patients to answer questions and alleviate fears associated with medications they were taking. I realized relief from pain and nausea are great blessings to those trying to comfortably and peacefully live out their remaining days.

Over the years I've counseled patients, laughed with them, cried with them, reassured them of God's presence, and prayed with them. And I can still hear Sue's words to a young "rookie" pharmacist who thought she was too cool for a job that desperately needed her knowledge and compassion. When there are days that are too long, feet that are hurting, shoulders that are burdened with the weight of others, I am hopeful I can spread a smile to a stranger's face as I try in some small way to minister to their heart.

BREAKROOM BOOST

Sometimes the work of our peers can seem so much more important than the seemingly lackluster aspects of our own day-to-day jobs. But the work we do as Christ-followers is for an upside-down Kingdom, in which a small lunch of loaves and fishes feeds thousands, in which the widow's mite means more than millions, in which the ninety-nine are left behind to find the one.

HANDWASHING PRAYER

When I get bogged down with the monotonous and lackluster parts of my job, Lord, help me remember what a privilege it is to do the smallest things that mean the world to my patients.

Record today's fears, frustrations, and heartbreak:

_____

_____

_____

_____

EVIDENCE-BASED HOPE

Record things you are grateful for and where you've seen God working this week:

_____

_____

_____

_____

DAY 11

Wash me, and I will be whiter than snow.

PSALM 51:7

Henry Mitchell was about as dejected a patient as I'd seen in some time. Clad in overalls that hung from his aging frame, he slumped in the wheelchair the triage nurse, Michelle, had used to catch him as his knee buckled and he crumpled into a sagging heap. His wife, Jean, wasn't in much better shape. In fact, for a moment I wondered which one was the patient.

"Hi, Mr. Mitchell, I'm Anne. I'll be your nurse this afternoon." He didn't look up, so I crouched to eye level with him. As I did so, the scent of stale urine was overwhelming. "What brings you here today?"

He lifted only his eyes, as if he were ashamed. "My knee."

"He had a knee replacement a couple of weeks ago," Michelle offered. "He thinks it might be infected."

"I *know* it's infected," he said, a touch of anger in his voice.

I looked up at his wife, standing behind him. She was shaking her head in disagreement, but in a way I knew all too well from patients' family members that meant Henry Mitchell wasn't telling the full story.

Henry looked up at me, and I noticed tears puddled in his rheumy eyes. "I can't get myself clean."

"Pardon me?" I said, glancing from Henry to Jean and back again. The urine odor was beginning to make sense.

"Tell 'er," he said to his wife.

Jean launched into a long description of her increasing pain and failing health and the fact that they didn't have a walk-in shower, only one in a bathtub Henry couldn't climb into, even with two good knees. He hadn't had a shower or a bath since he'd been home from the outpatient center that performed his knee surgery. He was too healthy for home health, and too weak to take care of himself.

As a trauma nurse, personal hygiene was the furthest thing from my mind. We treated acute problems like heart attacks and bowel blockages, wounds that needed stitches, and bouts of pneumonia that needed anti-biotics, and we sent the patients out the door or upstairs to the ward. But Henry was different. He needed more.

"Hold on a minute. I'll be right back." I winked at his wife.

I gathered towels and washcloths, and the unit secretary called one of the wards to send down soap and shampoo, shaving cream and a razor—supplies we didn't stock. My coworkers and I wheeled him into the decontamination showers usually reserved for chemical spills or other hazardous situations. We let the water run hot to steam up the room for added warmth. After peeling off Henry's filthy dungarees, we—along with Jean—sudsed him up and scrubbed him down.

When we were finished, I confirmed that his knee was healing properly and then helped him wiggle into a clean white T-shirt from a donation bin. As he pushed his arms through, he grabbed me by the hand.

"Thank you," he said, tears of a different kind in his eyes.

BREAKROOM BOOST
The ugliest parts of our hearts, the private places we can't reach on our own—those are the very ones God wants us to wheel before him, the ones he wants to lather and rinse and heal, just as he wants us to touch and clean others. No thought, no deed, no brokenness is beyond the reach of our Savior. Heroes don't hold back. Let him heal and clean those places in you, so that you can better care for others.

HANDWASHING PRAYER
Lord, thank you for the parts of my days that lead to unexpected blessings. Help me to see inconveniences as opportunities.

VITAL SIGNS

Record today's fears, frustrations, and heartbreak:

_____

_____

_____

_____

_____

EVIDENCE-BASED HOPE

Record things you are grateful for and where you've seen God working this week:

_____

_____

_____

_____

_____

DAY 12

"My thoughts are nothing like your thoughts," says the LORD.
"And my ways are far beyond anything you could imagine."
ISAIAH 55:8

I walk by the hallway mirror and notice my eyeliner is smeared, emphasized by the dark, under-eye circles I tried hard to hide with concealer this morning. The two remaining hours of my shift feel like an eternity. One more set of vital signs on my five needy patients. One more round of ice waters and medications and last-minute lab draws and stat add-on orders. And incessant call lights in between all that.

Does what I do even matter?

The days are so long, and every time I come to work, all I can think about is my next day off, when I can wake my children with a kiss and shepherd them, sleepy-headed, from breakfast to toothbrushing, to backpack gathering, to the school bus, where I can hug and kiss them goodbye and tell them I love them. My next day off, when I can crawl back into bed and sleep off the hangover-like exhaustion of the three twelve-hour shifts I just worked, so that I could have four uninterrupted days with my family. My next day off, when maybe I will feel clean enough and alive enough to give myself to my husband and love him with my whole heart and body.

I used to be able to focus on my patients for these twelve hours. For years, I could manage and balance the demands of my workdays and my home days. But most days now, my temper is short. I'm annoyed at the replacement staff before they even arrive. And on top of that, I've been assigned to the room at the end of the hall.

You know the room, Lord, the one where the same hospice patient has been lingering for three days, no family to speak of. His room is dark in the morning when I arrive, and I change his pads and linens, and turn him to his left, and tuck an extra pillow under his sacrum where the bedsore will never heal and between the bones of his knobby knees, the flesh of his unmoving thighs hopeless and sagging.

I turn him again, two hours later.

And again, two hours after that.

Every two hours, I turn him.

Never does he move, except for the rise and fall of his chest, and I am most grateful.

I just want to make it out of here before he dies, after all.

I just want to get home.

What good am I to him—to anyone—really?

BREAKROOM BOOST

God does know that patient at the end of the hall. And he knows you. He saw when you stayed beside the dying man for a moment after pushing that most recent dose of morphine. He saw you run your fingers across the ropey-veined, pale hand, still warm with life but unmoving, with death looming heavy. You thought it was the morphine that eased his breathing. It did, to some extent. But what settled the restless gasps even more was your touch. God's touch. Through you. God used you then, and he will use you again. His light shines best through brokenness.

HANDWASHING PRAYER

Lord, help me trust that you are always working, even when I can't see or feel you, and in spite of my weariness.

VITAL SIGNS

Record today's fears, frustrations, and heartbreak:

_____

_____

_____

_____

_____

Record things you are grateful for and where you've seen God working this week:

_____

_____

_____

_____

_____

DAY 13

Even when I walk through the darkest valley,
I will not be afraid.
PSALM 23:4

Six-year-old Sadie had been coming to our pediatric hospital emergency department multiple times a year since she was an infant. Plagued by a congenital metabolic disorder, she had already lived years beyond what physicians had predicted, no doubt because of the mother's meticulous dedication to administering her medications as often as every fifteen minutes throughout the day and night.

When her mother rushed her in during a February ice storm, we knew immediately from Sadie's color and breathing that she was in worse condition than she'd ever been. Her low oxygen levels rose a bit when we applied and turned up the oxygen. Her heart stopped, but within a few compressions restarted. However, she never regained consciousness.

The parents consulted for what seemed like hours with Sadie's physicians. Through the window of that room, I could see them wiping tears, the father holding the mother, the two of them nodding as the physicians spoke.

I busied myself with triaging other children in the emergency department, even as I kept my eye on Sadie. Someone had turned on the video she had always loved of happy, healthy children singing classic Bible songs.

Eventually, the family decided they would let her go. The IV and most of the monitors were removed and silenced. The video was turned off too. Family gathered around, passing her from one set of loving arms to the other.

"Give her back to me," her mother said to the father. "She needs to die in my arms."

The physician came back into the room and gently caressed Sadie's tousled blonde hair. "We can take the oxygen off now," he said.

The remaining heart monitor read thirty beats per minute. It wouldn't be long now.

Reluctant to take her eyes off Sadie's face, the mother looked up at him. "Will it hurt her? Will she suffer?"

"No," he said. "She is in a different place now."

The physician nodded to me, and I gently removed the oxygen cannula from around her face and head. I turned off the hissing oxygen valve and shut down the last glaring monitor.

Her tears falling on Sadie's soft, pale cheeks, the mother kissed her daughter. "It's okay, Sadie, you can go to Jesus now."

Sadie took one last breath and was gone.

By the end of my shift, the ice storm had passed and the sun sank below the horizon, leaving behind a burst of fuchsia and orange light.

BREAKROOM BOOST

Even when anticipated, the loss of someone under our care can make us feel that we failed the patient, the family, even our coworkers. What if we had tried one more medication? One more round of chemotherapy? One more attempt at transplant? Five more minutes of chest compressions? The what-ifs march through our minds. And yet, moments surrounding death are what nursing is about. It's not as much about saving as it is about loving. Not just about monitors or medication titration, but about who we are inside, and what we can do to help patients and their families. It's about patients like Sadie, for whom the best we can do is to help them slip peacefully into the arms of their Savior.

HANDWASHING PRAYER

Lord, sometimes I see so much death at work that it hurts. Please come and recenter my grieving, aching heart.

VITAL SIGNS

Record today's fears, frustrations, and heartbreak:

_____

_____

_____

_____

EVIDENCE-BASED HOPE

Record things you are grateful for and where you've seen God working this week:

_____

_____

_____

_____

DAY 14

Nothing in all creation is hidden from God.
Everything is naked and exposed before his eyes.
HEBREWS 4:13

Three hundred and six kilograms.

I blinked at the screen and the numbers on the electronic medical record. My kilograms-to-pounds conversion skills relied heavily on a calculator, but I didn't have to convert this number to know the gravity of the weight.

As I approached the room, I could hear his nurse chatting cheerily with him as she went about her work of administering his medications, assessing, and moving the twenty-eight-year-old man. When I walked into the room, I didn't know what to expect, but it definitely was not what I saw. Blue eyes sunken into fleshy cheeks studied me as I tried not to gape and fixate on the massive frame around him. His arms looked as if they were draped with balloons of fabric. His trunk and abdomen filled the largest bariatric bed available, one the hospital had to special-order.

"Hey, Henry, how are you?" I said, moving toward the bed. When I glanced at his face, his cheeks were splattered with pink that I worried was from shame. Undoubtedly, he was used to being seen more for his body than his heart, his soul.

As his case manager, even before I met him I was having a hard time finding a way to get him discharged. He could not return to his home. His mother was in poor health, and he needed constant support for even the most basic activities of daily living: bathing, food preparation, dressing, moving. Rural home health agencies in his part of the state had recently stopped taking Medicaid patients. He required lift machines and extra staff because of his size, which limited the number of extended-care facilities that could accommodate him.

"I just want to go home," he said, his thin and shaky voice taking me by surprise.

"I know, I'm trying," I assured in vain.

In the realm of discharge planning, my hands were proverbially tied.

I grabbed his hand, skin stretched smooth, in mine. Government insurance and regulations made me feel like a hamster running on a wheel I could never hop off, never being able to help the people who needed it the most.

The nurse finished her work and left the room, and I pulled the sheet over him and tucked it under his chin, covering his hugeness but not the enormity of the situation. My mind wandered to blame—how could he let himself get like this? Where had his parents been? Why couldn't he just stop eating so much?

Conviction came in waves as I realized I had my own deep rolls of shame, my own overgrown panniculus of regrets, my own heart hurts I hid behind overspending or the bottle of wine I drank every night or the irreverent laughter with my coworkers. Who but this man knew the kind of pain he had faced as a child, the kind of neglect, abandonment, abuse—the kind of life he'd led before he reached this impossible moment?

How different were he and I, really?

BREAKROOM BOOST

We are so good at pulling on our scrubs, clipping on our name tags, and focusing on saving others. How easily we forget how much we, too, need to be saved every moment of every day. No number of shifts worked, no years of tenure, no level of management can hide how desperately we, too, need a healer. God sees it all—your pain and your patients' pain. No matter where you go, what you do, how you look, God sees you and he loves you still.

HANDWASHING PRAYER

Lord, search my heart. Reveal my pain. Help me overcome my dependence on anything but you.

Record today's fears, frustrations, and heartbreak:

_____

_____

_____

_____

EVIDENCE-BASED HOPE

Record things you are grateful for and where you've seen God working this week:

_____

_____

_____

_____

DAY 15

Let your conversation be gracious and attractive so that you will have the right response for everyone.

COLOSSIANS 4:6

"*Cómo estás hoy*, Señor Garcia?" I smiled at the man lying still on the bed. I was grateful to have taken those required Spanish classes in college that I had complained about so many times.

Señor Garcia blinked, the corners of his eyes crinkling, a sign we all knew was his way of telling us he was doing okay. A roofing worker for over twenty years in the United States, he'd gotten used to not harnessing in on even the steepest roofs. But a misplaced, unseen nail gun was all it took to send him careening two and a half stories to the ground, landing on the back of his neck, rendering him a quadriplegic for life. After 287 days, we had all learned how to communicate with him, whether Spanish or eye-blinking. Most of all, we were acutely aware of his desire to go home to his family in Mexico. An undocumented immigrant, he had no insurance, which meant no place to discharge to since he was now reliant upon a tracheostomy and a ventilator.

On his bedside table was a framed photograph of his family in Mexico: a mother, two brothers, three sisters, and a host of nieces and nephews to whom he had sent most of his paychecks over the years.

Our entire unit had become attached to Señor Garcia over the weeks and months, even arranging a birthday party (complete with a piñata we hit for him). Whether we were throwing him a party, arranging telephone calls to his family, or lingering after his morning care to make sure he was comfortable, he always responded with tears of gratitude running down his temples.

As I was caring for Señor Garcia's tracheostomy tube, the phone rang in my pocket. It was the nurses' station.

"It's Mr. Barrett," the unit secretary said. "He's asking why you haven't been in to give him his discharge paperwork yet."

Mr. Barrett had a star by his chart, indicating he was a VIP. Staff know the star means we will often be faced with demanding, ungrateful patients and family members who aren't used to waiting for anything, let alone for a busy nurse to attend to them. He would want his paperwork immediately, paperwork that took time to do well and accurately.

I closed my eyes and sighed. In my mind, I cursed. But one glance at Señor Garcia reminded me that I had a choice about how I responded to difficult situations, difficult patients. "I'll be there as soon as I can."

Friends ask me if I get tired of working in the city hospital, and sometimes I do, but not for the reasons they might assume. The extremes of caring for grateful patients like Señor Garcia who have nothing, and the Mr. Barretts who are here for three days and gone leave me exasperated and discouraged. Here at the city hospital, it's easy to see why Jesus taught that the last will be first. I do my best to hurry, reminding myself that as frustrating as he is, Mr. Barrett is made in God's image too.

BREAKROOM BOOST

Birth and death. Remission and recurrence. Gratitude and attitude. The daily whiplash of diverse situations can make us feel like anything but a hero. There's so little time to process, let alone realize that there is a time for everything before moving on or being shoved into the next admission, the next critical lab result, the next code blue. But like a sunrise, God's love rises new every morning to give us grace to handle the extremes we face every day.

HANDWASHING PRAYER

Lord, help me keep my eyes on you. Calm my heart that feels so unmoored by the often extreme and constantly changing situations at work.

Record today's fears, frustrations, and heartbreak:

_____

_____

_____

_____

EVIDENCE-BASED HOPE

Record things you are grateful for and where you've seen God working this week:

_____

_____

_____

_____

DAY 16

You are royal priests, a holy nation, God's very own possession.
As a result, you can show others the goodness of God.
1 PETER 2:9

New Orleans is known for its music, its food, and its tendency to attract disasters, so when COVID-19 arrived, it was no surprise that we were hit hard. Young or old, preexisting risk factors or perfectly healthy, no one was spared from the virus's haphazard, unpredictable patterns.

Because many of the hospital chaplains were elderly, they were not allowed to visit patients and families during the worst days of the pandemic, a time when chaplains were needed the most. Death after sudden death, intense grief, and overwhelming fear created a vortex of emotional exhaustion for patients, families, and staff alike.

As the chief nursing officer of the hospital, I try to round on all the floors at least once a week, and more than that if time allows. One morning I headed to the nurses' station of the medical unit we had designated for confirmed or suspected COVID-19 patients. The heartbreak there was palpable as soon as I went through the double doors, which were covered in signs that warned about the required personal protective equipment and stringent no-visitor policy.

My phone rang, and it was my administrative assistant. "I have the mother of one of the patients on the line. Can you take the call?"

"Of course. Put her through."

I listened to the mother of Kevin, whom she described as an outgoing young man who loved his work as a pharmaceutical salesman. He'd contracted the virus at a conference on the East Coast, and within forty-eight hours he was in the intensive care unit, ventilated. She hadn't been able to communicate with him since.

I kept listening as Kevin's mother continued, and pointed to his name on the assignment sheet at the desk. I looked at the ICU charge nurse, and she knew without a word that I was asking if there was any hope for him.

She shook her head.

Kevin's mom paused on the other end of the line, then asked in a voice cracking with emotion, "Will you please pray with my son? I don't think he's going to make it."

"I will," I said. "And I will make sure he does not die alone."

I canceled my afternoon meetings. Using an iPad with his mother present via video call, I stayed with Kevin and did the best I could to comfort him as he quickly deteriorated. I set the iPad by his pillow, and his mother told him over and over how much she loved him, how proud she was, how the biggest gift of her life was being his mother.

His breathing slowed and his blood pressure fell, and I began to pray in earnest. Staff who had a moment prayed outside the room with us. I don't even know what I said. But I will always remember that Kevin's mom and I were both praying for him when he took his last breath.

BREAKROOM BOOST

If healthcare workers are anything, we are resourceful. A title is often just that, replaced as needed by *waitress*, *barber*, and the various roles of coworkers when they are indisposed. We didn't set out to be heroes. We just keep showing up. And by God's grace, he uses us to be his hands and feet.

HANDWASHING PRAYER

Lord, clear the calendar of my heart and show me how to serve as you would serve, in whatever capacity I am called to today.

VITAL SIGNS

Record today's fears, frustrations, and heartbreak:

_____

_____

_____

_____

Record things you are grateful for and where you've seen God working this week:

_____

_____

_____

_____

DAY 17

You will always have the poor among you.

MATTHEW 26:11

I crossed my arms and buried my head in them. A two-inch-thick stack of psychosocial assessments, pending Medicaid applications, and FMLA paperwork cushioned the desk as I focused on breathing in, breathing out.

For days I'd been fielding questions and demands from physicians, residents, charge nurses, and administration about why Mr. Martin was still on our unit. A stubborn and cantankerous man, he had been admitted for a revision of his tracheostomy as an outpatient-in-a-bed. He should have discharged the next day, and medically he could have. But eight days later, he was still here, stalled because the only place Mr. Martin could—or would—discharge to was his tent underneath the bridge by the canal that ran through the center of the city.

Surgical residents—the ones in charge of the final discharge—refused to write a release order until I, the assigned social worker, could arrange what they deemed a "safe discharge." They were concerned about his tracheostomy—one the patient had been living with independently for over fifteen years. Newly revised, surely it would get infected or worse at the homeless camp, and no home-healthcare agency would service him there. But there were no other options. I wasn't able to produce a furnished apartment with the rent paid and pantry stocked.

The charge nurse didn't care where he went; she just wanted him gone. Her staff were understandably exasperated with caring for him. Much too healthy to be here, Mr. Martin roamed restlessly around the halls and had frequent outbursts of frustration of his own. Visitors from his tent village crammed into his room at mealtimes, when he ordered twice the amount of food necessary so he could share with them.

The idealistic part of me felt like a failure for my inability to find Mr. Martin any place other than his tent. The seasoned social worker part of me knew that finding homes for the homeless, insurance for the uninsured, and safe spaces for the abused was not only unrealistic, but impossible. And the human, heart part of me knew Mr. Martin would be just fine in the tent village.

Eventually, the surgery team realized there was no other choice.

Discharge orders finally written, I entered his room with a grin. "Good news, Mr. Martin. You're going home."

Unsure of what my ever-changing definition of *home* for him was, he eyed me suspiciously.

"I'm arranging a Medicaid cab to take you home. Back to your tent. Back to your friends."

"My *family*," he corrected.

"Your family." I nodded.

We tried not to erupt into cheers when Mr. Martin left the unit, a hospital-issued bag of his few belongings and extra trach-care supplies in one hand, and another full of fruit and other food he'd saved from his trays in the other. Pausing at the nurses' station, he pulled the tracheostomy tube from his stoma, tossed it at the reluctant resident, and sauntered off with a smile.

Mr. Martin was going to be just fine.

BREAKROOM BOOST

As caregivers, our nature is to fix, heal, and rescue. But only Christ can change a heart. Our best efforts, even if unheeded, are not wasted. The seeds we plant in the lives of our patients may lay dormant under thick, loamy layers of mulch. The watering, tending, and exposure to the sun is the work of the Master Gardener. Though he wants no one to perish, he forces his way on no one. And we, on the front lines, are called only to do the best we can with what we have and release the rest to Jesus.

Lord, when my efforts feel vain and wasted, remind me that I am simply called to do the best I can with what I have.

VITAL SIGNS

Record today's fears, frustrations, and heartbreak:

_____

_____

_____

_____

_____

_____

_____

_____

EVIDENCE-BASED HOPE

Record things you are grateful for and where you've seen God working this week:

_____

_____

_____

_____

_____

_____

_____

_____

DAY 18

He will gently lead the mother sheep with their young.

ISAIAH 40:11

"**G**ood morning, sunshine," I cooed to my eighteen-month-old daughter, Hannah, as I walked into the nursery I'd painted soft pink. Outside her window, the darkness showed no signs of morning. Only my watch confirmed it, the one I used at work to count respirations and heart rates and the hours until I could come home to her again. The plump pout of her lower lip and the fast-forming tears in her eyes were the last thing I'd expected from my usually happy girl.

I collected her in my arms and took her to the changing table. "What's wrong, baby girl?"

She pointed to my blue scrub top, lip trembling all the more.

My work wasn't something that had bothered her before, but staff shortages and COVID-19 were fast altering all our lives, requiring my presence now more than ever as a unit manager. As I prepared for the fourth in a long line of twelve-hour shifts in the ICU, even Hannah had had enough of my extra work hours, of the way my husband had to hold her back so I could undress and shower before touching her.

"Oh, sweetie, I'm so sorry." I brushed away tears of my own as I secured her clean diaper, picked her up, and pulled her close. "You are my sunshine—" I began to sing, dancing with her as long as I could before I had to rush out the door.

"You need to go," my husband said as he came into the room. He wrapped Hannah and me in his arms and swayed along with us. His sleep-tousled hair made him all the more handsome and all the harder to leave this morning, and though it meant more pressure on me to pay the bills, I envied the fact that he was furloughed from his job with no sign of his company bringing him back any time soon.

"I'll take her," he said, beginning the difficult task of peeling Hannah from my arms.

Hannah's sniffling turned to wailing, and I felt the prick of tears in my own eyes as I looked at the two of them, my whole world, in that little pink nursery.

"It's okay, honey. Mama will be home soon," I lied.

Again.

As I pulled my car from the driveway, the news station listed the latest COVID-19 statistics. The crisis worsened by the day. My heart felt as foggy as the surroundings my headlights barely illuminated. The endless patients—vented and laid prone and dying—were taking a toll on even the most seasoned, calloused of ICU nurse hearts.

BREAKROOM BOOST

Whether our stresses stem from COVID-19, staff shortages, or unexpected spikes in patient census, the Lord knows we are weary. But he is with us. He is holding us and our families as we face this fight. He provides stones for our Goliaths, manna for our wilderness, and spring rain for our droughts. He is with us always.

HANDWASHING PRAYER

Lord, give me strength when I have none. Give me grace. And protect my loved ones as I care for the loved ones of others.

VITAL SIGNS

Record today's fears, frustrations, and heartbreak:

_____

_____

_____

_____

_____

_____

Record things you are grateful for and where you've seen God working this week:

_____

_____

_____

_____

_____

_____

DAY 19

God has not given us a spirit of fear and timidity, but of power, love, and self-discipline.
2 TIMOTHY 1:7

The day I had been dreading all semester finally came: the mental health clinical. As I prepared, I reminded myself to stay removed, stay objective. "Do not get overly invested in your patients, and do not view it personally if they have outbursts," my professor had cautioned. Not an easy assignment for a naive nursing student, let alone a believer.

The pediatric psychiatric unit was strictly structured, with different therapy groups, doctor appointments, and debriefing sessions. Initially, I could tell some of the kids were trying to act cool, to laugh it off as they shared their painful stories. I'd been their age a short time before, and I remembered all too well the importance of maintaining a facade of "having it all together." But it didn't take long for one of them to get mad or break down in sobs.

I sat in shock as these kids described situations no one should ever have to face: abuse of every kind, addictions, eating disorders, suicidal thoughts, abandonment, panic attacks, feelings of complete and utter worthlessness with no desire to live.

At lunch I sat by a willowy girl with sunken cheeks who refused to touch her food, telling me she was too fat to eat.

I played Jenga with another, blue streak of color in her hair, crude piercings across her brow and upper lip, her arms covered in cuts and scars.

A young man, broad-shouldered and dressed in high-end clothing, looked as if he could be captain of any high school football team. He told me that his father had abandoned the family and that he didn't want to be here anymore.

Story after heart-wrenching story broke my heart into smaller and smaller pieces. What could I possibly do in a handful of nursing-student clinicals to make them believe that they are worthy, that they are loved? Who was I to them but a stranger? Every time I tried to offer words of encouragement, they came out sounding empty and forced.

Through frustration and tears I finally asked God what I could do, how I could help.

I took a deep breath and decided to just start talking about what I knew: soccer.

Before long, half a dozen of the teens sat in a circle with me, bantering back and forth about Manchester United and Arsenal, and the recent US Women's soccer team accomplishments. The whole atmosphere in the room changed—or was it just my heart? Without the pressure of trying to "fix" them, the conversation turned to what they enjoyed, what they were passionate about. In the midst of that, I noticed their eyes lighting up with life.

BREAKROOM BOOST

Reaching the wounds and diseases of the mind feels like crossing a minefield, each step toward the patient filled with apprehension and the risk that we will trigger an explosive reaction. And yet, when we can't see where it hurts on an X-ray or MRI, God knows just the spot that needs healing. Our presence with a patient, our assignment for the day, is no coincidence. We have something our patients need, even if it's something simple like sharing about the soccer we played or the garden we tend or the painting we do on the side.

HANDWASHING PRAYER

Lord, thank you for the variety of experiences in my life. Help me recognize when I can use them to bring joy and connection to a broken heart.

VITAL SIGNS

Record today's fears, frustrations, and heartbreak:

_____

_____

_____

_____

EVIDENCE-BASED HOPE

Record things you are grateful for and where you've seen God working this week:

_____

_____

_____

_____

DAY 20

You have closed their minds to understanding,
but do not let them triumph.
JOB 17:4

I pushed room 201's door open and took stock of the patient and the two friends sitting beside him. It wasn't the first time I'd been floated to the adult unit from my job of twenty-five years on the pediatric unit, and I made a mental checklist of the differences adult patients required.

I became acutely aware that the voices that had been so jovial moments before had grown silent, and I felt the heat of their stares.

"Hi, my name is Nevaeh. I'll be your nurse today." I focused on adding my name to the whiteboard, including RN at the end, and copying the vital signs onto the papers on my clipboard.

When I turned around, the patient and his friends stared at me with eyebrows raised in apparent confusion.

"Is something wrong?" I asked.

"You said you're the *nurse*?" one asked, voice thick with sarcasm.

"Yes. I'm his nurse for this evening," I said matter-of-factly, then turned to the patient. "Is it okay if I assess you? Or would you prefer that I come back later?"

His friends began to question me.

"Lemme see that badge," the other friend said, taking a step toward me, reaching out and flicking the bright red tag with the RN on it. He sniggered. "Where's your license?"

My stomach twisted.

The accusatory questions continued, and eventually the second man picked up the phone and dialed the hospital operator. "Yeah, this is room 201. We need security up here. There's an unidentified Black woman who won't show us her license."

I prayed they couldn't see the fury rising in my chest, and I nervously tugged at the stethoscope—the one my mama bought me for my second graduation—hanging around my neck.

"You have any arrest warrants?" the other friend asked, grinning at the one using the phone.

I stepped back and offered my own question to the patient, one I've had to ask too many times to count. "Sir, would you feel more comfortable with a Caucasian nurse? If so, I would be more than happy to get a changed assignment for you."

The man in the bed looked me in my eyes, turned and looked at his friends, then looked slowly up and down my body. "No, sweetheart. You're just fine with me. You're a pretty colored gal."

With that, I left the room, tears flooding my eyes. I passed the hospital security guards and the charge nurse heading my way.

"You need backup in 201?" a voice questioned on the crackling walkie-talkie of one of the officers.

I collapsed onto the couch in the breakroom. In my twenty-five years of taking care of children with skin of every shade, they have mispronounced my name, coughed on me, peed on me, pulled my hair, and pinched me, but not one of them has ever doubted my abilities, asked for my license, or called security on me. Sure, their parents eyed me, but in moments of sickness, they generally refrained from behaving the way these men did.

I knew in my head not much has changed in the way of prejudice these days.

I guess I just keep hoping it will.

BREAKROOM BOOST

As incredible as it sounds, this story is based on nearly identical events that happened in 1976 and in 2020. As healthcare workers, we need to be especially sensitive to the challenges faced by coworkers and patients alike that arise from racial or cultural prejudice, and to speak out when we find ourselves the subject of such prejudice. Together, we can strive to create synchrony instead of suspicion, an inclusive future, and a just and loving workplace where healing is blind to everything except empathy and love.

HANDWASHING PRAYER

I'm so tired of the hate, Lord. Help me see places where I can be a light in the darkest places of this world.

VITAL SIGNS

Record today's fears, frustrations, and heartbreak:

_____

_____

_____

_____

EVIDENCE-BASED HOPE

Record things you are grateful for and where you've seen God working this week:

_____

_____

_____

_____

DAY 21

You have turned my mourning into joyful dancing.

PSALM 30:11

Life's a dance, so they say. And nowhere is this more evident than in years spent working the wards of a small county hospital, where generations come and go. Walls yellowed with age even white paint can't cover, the forte of births balance with the slow, pianissimo waltz of death.

The previous year, I had cared for Maude. Legs swollen with the edema of end-stage heart failure, she recited story after story of God's provision on their family farm, all the while beaming at her husband of sixty-four years, Gil, who sat at her side, leaving only to shower and grab a bite to eat in the morning. Embraced by Gil, Maude passed in her sleep one night, just before I arrived for my day shift.

Now Gil was my patient. In and out of the hospital since Maude's passing, he was now gravely ill, and had changed his status to "Do Not Resuscitate."

One evening when his breathing had become labored and his lab tests and vital signs pointed to pending death, I spent a little extra time with him. We both knew I was saying goodbye.

"I can't wait to see Maude," he grinned with the last remnants of the schoolboy he once was.

I marveled at his peace, unsure if I would feel the same way when faced with death.

"Give her a hug for me, will you?" I asked.

"Of course," he nodded.

I kissed him on the top of his head.

Twelve hours later, I expected his room to be empty and cleaned, if not occupied with a new patient altogether. But there he was.

"What are you still doing here?" I teased. "You were supposed to be dancing with Maude by now."

"I was waiting for you." He winked.

I performed his morning assessment and got him set up for

breakfast, then moved on to my other patients. When I was in the last room, I noticed the unit secretary hovering outside the door.

"Come look. You have to see this," she said, leading me to Gil's room.

He sat exactly the way I'd left him, but the rattled, labored breathing and weary eyes had been replaced by an ethereal peace, furrowed brow smoothed and face softened with the peace of death and no doubt the joy of dancing with Maude.

BREAKROOM BOOST

Always looming but seldom addressed in our modern society, death is sterilized and postponed and fiercely battled in vain. Each of us began the march toward the grave at birth, and often as healthcare workers we are positioned as players in an endgame we can never win. The quandary of our hero hearts is that of all people, we have the ability and privilege to make death peaceful and beautiful. Mourning turns to dancing not because we cease to grieve, but because we realize that in death the true and eternal dance begins.

HANDWASHING PRAYER

Lord, help me bring comfort, peace, and even joy to the dying.

VITAL SIGNS

Record today's fears, frustrations, and heartbreak:

_____

_____

_____

_____

_____

_____

Record things you are grateful for and where you've seen God working this week:

_____

_____

_____

_____

_____

_____

DAY 22

Don't worry about anything; instead, pray about everything.
Tell God what you need, and thank him for all he has done.
PHILIPPIANS 4:6

Thud. The floor outside room 220 shook with the force of the sound, and my stomach lurched as I ran into the room.

"Mr. Kowalski!" His half-naked body was sprawled on the floor, limbs at impossible angles. "Shanice! Carrie! I need some help in here!"

My colleagues arrived, breathless, and knelt alongside me and Mr. Kowalski, the three of us trying to untangle the twisted IV lines, oxygen tubing, and hospital gown. A gash above his right eye and a large skin tear on his left arm dripped blood, along with a hole in the bend of his right arm where the IV had been inserted.

If I told him once, I told him a hundred times not to get up without our help. "Mr. Kowalski, what were you thinking?"

He looked up at me with fear and shame in his eyes.

"Let's get you cleaned up now," Shanice soothed as she pulled him into a sitting position.

Taylor, the charge nurse, joined us with a stack of fresh linens and a new gown, and together the four of us spent nearly an hour cleaning, bathing, bandaging, salving, calling physicians and radiology to arrange precautionary X-rays, and finally fluffing the pillow on which Mr. Kowalski could lay his battered head.

Carrie pulled the new sheet and coverlet over his legs and chest as Shanice ran a comb through his disheveled hair. "There. Now you look handsome."

I placed the call light in his cool, ropey-veined hand, but he set it aside and began cleaning his foggy glasses with the edge of the coverlet. When he was through, he set them on his face, revealing how crooked they'd become in the fall.

His eyes moistened as he looked up at me. "I just wanted to go to the bathroom. By myself."

I took a second and tried to imagine what it would be like to have to rely on someone all the time to help me go to the bathroom. I thought about how up until the last couple of weeks, Mr. Kowalski had spent the better part of eighty-three years taking care of his own personal business.

Setting my hand on his shoulder, I thought about all the times I rushed to do something I knew might not have the best consequences, how many times I had suffered my own shameful fall from grace for forging ahead with my own stubborn plans without waiting to ask God what he thought about my decisions. I thought about how gracious the Lord has been to not holler "I told you so" in my ear.

"I understand, Mr. Kowalski. I really do. It's hard to rely on others for things you've always done yourself. It's hard to let yourself be helped, to let others help you. It's hard for me, too."

BREAKROOM BOOST

Anxiety and impatience plague our lives more than we realize, often causing us to prioritize task lists over doing the right thing. Fierce independence is wired into our healthcare-trained hearts. We don't have time to wait for a coworker to double-check an armband or medication dose, the temptation to get things done pressing and all too real. Pandemic and compassion fatigue only make things worse. And yet we need coworkers to keep us from making mistakes or worse. Practicing self-care on your day off and checking your heart and the hearts of your friends are two tangible ways to combat this constant struggle. It's okay to not be okay, and it's important to ask for help when you need it.

HANDWASHING PRAYER

Lord, help me remember to not worry about anything, and not to take matters into my own hands that I ought to wait for.

Record today's fears, frustrations, and heartbreak:

_____

_____

_____

_____

EVIDENCE-BASED HOPE
Record things you are grateful for and where you've seen God working this week:

_____

_____

_____

_____

DAY 23

I, yes I, am the one who comforts you.

ISAIAH 51:12

"**I** want a new nurse." The elderly woman scowled at me from her hospital bed. She was careful to glare without moving her head, lest she disturb the nasogastric tube precariously taped and secured to her nose.

I wanted to celebrate.

I did celebrate, at least on the outside, joking with my coworkers about how glad I was to be "fired" from her care. She was a frequent flyer, admitting to our floor every few weeks for tweaks to her hydration and electrolytes, antibiotics for relentless urinary tract infections, and numerous other conditions that her failing body was unable to manage without the acute assistance hospitalization provided. And such patients are, to say the least, high maintenance.

Caregivers become exhausted from tending to needs and conditions of the never-ending admissions that can never be completely assuaged or cured. We draw straws—or rather, acquiesce to the charge nurse's desperate decision—about which nurse will be assigned to the frequent flyer for the day.

These patients are exhausted—and exasperated—by strangers who can't ever seem to manage their pain or their bowels or their desperation at wanting to be anywhere but in that bed, staring up at us.

Still, when she fired me, I felt like a failure.

I'd woken up that morning, pulled on my extra-soft scrubs, and driven to work listening to praise music, determined to give my best and my all to my patients.

I'd accepted the assignment of this frequent flyer that morning, confident I could make a difference for her that day, even looking forward to the challenge of making her content for the twelve hours she would be my responsibility. Together we would have a good day, she and I, nasogastric tube and all. I would deliver her medications on time, anticipate her pain medication needs before she had to ask, keep her cup of ice chips full, care for her paper-thin skin so she would not acquire a sore. Not on my shift.

And yet, midmorning, the patient requested a new nurse without warning, without any identifying provocation, without reason except that I was not enough.

When I told the charge nurse, she rearranged room assignments with a seasoned laugh and an eye roll, and I joined her.

On the outside.

But on the inside, I wondered if I would . . . if I could . . . ever be enough.

BREAKROOM BOOST

God heard the patient's words when she asked for a new nurse. But he also saw her heart. He saw a memory from fifty years ago stirring from deep within her, sunlight spilling through tree limbs to form a dappled pattern. He saw the man who would become her husband, strong armed and smelling of Aqua Velva, who sat beside her on a green grassy hill, underneath the limbs of that great oak. Memory stirred within her of being able to rise from the ground without effort, to feel her husband's arms around her without wincing in pain, to taste the wine and fresh French bread of their picnic without her gut seizing with cramps, and to dance without a thought of incontinence. It was the youth she saw that reminded her of these things, and it was her own grief and longing she wanted to beat out of the room and out of her life. We have not failed in such situations. Our patients seek a comfort only God can give.

HANDWASHING PRAYER

Lord, help me focus on you when I feel incompetent. And comfort the patients I cannot comfort.

Record today's fears, frustrations, and heartbreak:

_____

_____

_____

_____

EVIDENCE-BASED HOPE

Record things you are grateful for and where you've seen God working this week:

_____

_____

_____

_____

DAY 24

A real friend sticks closer than a brother.

PROVERBS 18:24

"**S**ee ya later!" I said to my friends from the emergency department as we parted ways leaving the hospital cafeteria. After fifteen years as a unit secretary there, it had been a hard but necessary decision to take a new job in the dietetics department. Working traumas together creates a deep connection between colleagues, after all. But with my son grown and myself barely over fifty, I was ready for a steady day job with a little less stress. Running into my friends and catching up over morning coffee makes it feel like I never left them.

I settled into my reports and phone calls, messages and task list for the day, and tried to ignore the burning in my chest.

"I'm going to have to do something about this heartburn," I said to Julie, the dietitian who shared our office.

"Giving up that extra-large coffee might help," she teased.

Suddenly I was overwhelmed with nausea. I grabbed the trash can under my desk just in time and gave up all the coffee and more.

"Carrie!" Julie exclaimed. "Are you okay?"

I shook my head. I was not okay. I couldn't stop vomiting. This was no ordinary stomach pain. No ordinary nausea. I was beginning to sweat all over, and the pain was excruciating.

"Marsha—I need some help," Julie called to a coworker. She turned to me "Carrie, you look terrible. Your color—"

"I think—I think I need help," I said, now breathless in addition to all my other symptoms.

"I think you do too. Let's get you to the ER."

The ride in the wheelchair was a blur, except when the hospital administrator, also an old friend, caught up with us halfway there and said into a phone pressed to her ear, "Get a room ready. Mmm-hmmm. Carrie Rogers. It's looking cardiac to me."

I felt like I was in a dream as I watched my dear friends hook me up to an electrocardiogram, start an IV line, attach monitors, and determine that I was having a STEMI—an ST-Elevation Myocardial Infarction—the most emergent and deadly of heart attacks. Fear threatened to overwhelm me, but then Kris, my partner in crime when we worked complementing shifts as unit secretaries there—arrived at my side and grabbed my hand.

"We've got you, Carrie. We've got this. You've got this."

She didn't let go until minutes later, when the cardiac catheterization team transferred me to the procedure table in the cath lab.

The morphine and other medications I received calmed me somewhat as the team prepared me for the catheterization. I thought about my son and my sweet grandbaby, all the things I still wanted to do with them. I thought about how I'd been taking my health, my life, my days on the earth for granted.

Lord, let me live to see another day. Another week. Another year. Please let me live.

Three stents later, I woke up in the intensive care unit, my son and granddaughter by my side.

Thank you, Lord. Thank you, thank you, thank you.

Sixteen minutes is all it took, I found out later.

Sixteen minutes from the time I was wheeled into the emergency department, the STEMI identified, the team called, and the time the catheter guidewire reached the blockage threatening my life in my main cardiac artery.

The timing was a miracle.

That I was already in the hospital when the STEMI occurred was a miracle.

That I have friends like these is the best miracle of all.

I'm making some new friends now, octogenarians in cardiac rehabilitation. And it's true what they say: We get by with a little help from our friends.

BREAKROOM BOOST

Few things hurt the hearts of healthcare heroes more than when one of our own becomes a patient. Emotion threatens to overwhelm our adrenaline-driven, stoic, and professional responses. The bonds created through sharing sleepless nights and exhausting days, laughter and tears, and life and death are stronger than most any other. No matter how powerless we feel to make a difference for our patients, to get through a staffing crisis, or to overcome the fear of a deadly pandemic, our coworkers are always beside us. Whether we're dealing with a true cardiac emergency or the heartache of burnout, compassion fatigue, or moral injury, our work friends are often the best antidote of all.

HANDWASHING PRAYER

Few friends share the bond of healthcare friends. Thank you, Lord, for my friends.

VITAL SIGNS

Record today's fears, frustrations, and heartbreak:

_____

_____

_____

EVIDENCE-BASED HOPE

Record things you are grateful for and where you've seen God working this week:

_____

_____

_____

DAY 25

Thank God for this gift too wonderful for words!

2 CORINTHIANS 9:15

Colored string lights hung from the nurses' station, and an artificial tree covered in children's handmade ornaments stood in the corner when we got a call in the pediatric intensive care unit that they were bringing in a teenager by helicopter. Christopher had been opening Christmas gifts, his first one a pocketknife. They were a family of farmers, so this was a gift he'd been wanting for some time.

Christopher's second gift was a PlayStation gaming system. In his excitement, he used the pocketknife to cut off the heavy plastic strips around the box.

What happened next took the "You'll shoot your eye out" BB gun scene in the famous movie *A Christmas Story* to a whole new level.

The knife slipped, jamming straight into Christopher's chest. Instinctively, he pulled it straight back out. His parents took him to the local emergency department, and initially he was stable. However, his blood pressure began to drop quickly. His heart rate went up alarmingly. Scans revealed he had severed his mammary artery.

The transfer service let us know the patient would go straight to the operating room and then come to our unit. In the meantime, we prepared the room for his arrival.

I thought about my own teenagers opening presents that very morning, laughing and squealing with a year's worth of anticipation and excitement. The thought of that boy in the operating room, and his parents whom I imagined must be completely distraught, was so upsetting.

"Please, Lord, it's Christmas. No child should die because they were so excited opening presents celebrating your birthday."

While in surgery, Christopher required eight units of blood, but the surgeons were able to stabilize him. Just eight hours after he'd been opening Christmas presents, he reached our floor on a ventilator. Shortly thereafter, a volunteer brought the parents up to see him. They were clearly exhausted, and both had eyes red from worry, fear, and tears. As Christopher lay next to us, his chest rising and falling with the sounds of the ventilator, I explained all the equipment and our plans for care, and reassured them he was going to be okay.

"What questions do you have?" I asked.

His tearful mother asked me a few quiet, very appropriate questions.

Then his dad said, "I just have one question. Do y'all have a Walmart around here?"

After the day they had, I found this to be an odd question, but told them where the nearest store was.

His dad replied, "Great. Because we took off out of the house so fast I put on his mom's jeans."

We all laughed until our bellies ached.

Christopher came off the ventilator the next day, and was discharged home three days later.

It was a good Christmas after all.

BREAKROOM BOOST

Oh, the joy, when we can save a life and feel like we live up to the name "hero" at the end of a long shift, when we can enjoy an unexpected belly laugh with the release of gratitude and wonder and amazement—and discover that yes, the gift of life is too wonderful for words! Thank God our heartrending work is interspersed with these moments that make the hard ones worth fighting through and each shift another opportunity for hope. Just when we think no amount of grace can infuse us with the joy burnout has stolen, a patient like Christopher reminds us why we are called to do what we do.

HANDWASHING PRAYER

Lord, help me remember the patients I've had like Christopher when I feel weary and without hope.

Record today's fears, frustrations, and heartbreak:

_____

_____

_____

_____

EVIDENCE-BASED HOPE

Record things you are grateful for and where you've seen God working
this week:

_____

_____

_____

_____

DAY 26

He comforts us in all our troubles so that we can comfort others.
When they are troubled, we will be able to give them the same
comfort God has given us.

2 CORINTHIANS 1:4

"**O**ne month."

The words echoed in the room as I tried to choke back the tears. I was sitting in a seat no one, especially a nurse, ever wants to be in. I was the patient, and suddenly the diagnosis and the education I'd delivered to my own patients seemed a whole lot more real and scary.

The diagnosis of a hemorrhagic vocal polyp was long overdue. My voice had fluctuated with hoarseness for months before I finally decided to be examined.

"You'll require prednisone, vocal therapy, and strict vocal rest if there is any hope of recovery," the ear, nose, and throat specialist continued.

After he left, his nurse came in. She must have sensed my shock, because she pulled a chair up next to me and reached for my hands.

"You're going to get through this, Emily," she assured me. "And I'm going to tell you how."

She proceeded to spend the next hour with me, teaching me the details of why my silent sentence was so important.

I'm a nurse; shouldn't I have known all of this? I thought to myself. But all of my book knowledge meant nothing in that moment. I couldn't get enough of the information she so kindly offered. I couldn't get enough of her calm and assuring presence. By the time I left the clinic, I felt like I could see glimpses of hope in getting through this.

The month of restrictions commenced with awkward silence and alternative modes of communication including charades, typing countless phone notes, and mouthing out sentences while friends and family laughed and tried to decipher my new language. As time went by, I began to be acutely aware of things I otherwise would not have, like people who never seemed to stop talking, words and ideas tumbling out of their mouths without abandon. More interesting were the people I began to notice who hardly talked at all. In the midst of my sentence of silence,

I began to realize with a sweet new perspective the power of our words (and lack thereof).

Time and time again, I called upon the teaching that clinic nurse took the time to provide me. Her tips and encouragement got me through more than one moment of bitter discouragement. Most of all, I realized the significance of not only how we care for our patients, but how we teach them about the daily impact of a disease or condition on their lives. The importance of being present with each person gave patient education a whole new meaning.

BREAKROOM BOOST

One of the first things to go when fatigue and burnout threaten is the intentionality of seeing patients as the individuals they are. Asking about a patient's life, work, or family creates a paradigm shift from just getting through the day to identifying and treating the fear, apprehension, and grief of the situation. Even the most crotchety patient has been known to soften in the presence of a caregiver who braves what seems like endless moments of silence to draw out the deepest needs and brokenness.

HANDWASHING PRAYER

Lord, help me remember the significance of sitting, of listening first and talking last, and of taking time to give my patients the education they need.

VITAL SIGNS

Record today's fears, frustrations, and heartbreak:

_____

_____

_____

_____

Record things you are grateful for and where you've seen God working this week:

_____

_____

_____

_____

DAY 27

He will wipe every tear from their eyes, and
there will be no more death or sorrow or crying or pain.
All these things are gone forever.

REVELATION 21:4

We discharged a COVID-19 patient today.

COVID-19. The pandemic of all pandemics. The virus that brought all of us on the front lines to our knees with fear and uncertainty and even despair. Name a virus before this, and we knew how to combat it. Norovirus? Bring on the bleach. RSV? Bring on the PPE. Influenza? More PPE. Tuberculosis? Give us a negative-airflow room and N95 masks. All that and handwashing, and we were set.

We were warned in early 2020, and we waited. By March 2020, the COVID-19 patients began to arrive. We thought we were ready. In many ways, we were. Units and staffing were rearranged to accommodate increased ICU admissions. Supply chain administrators scrambled to adjust supply orders and distribution patterns.

And yet, nothing could have prepared us for the patients.

Old and young, poor and wealthy, those with never-ending comorbidity lists and those who had never been sick showed up on our wards. Oxygen-starved. Blood-clotting problems. Conflicting antidotes and anecdotes. Families saying goodbye through iPads and smartphones, and patients utterly alone.

But then came this day, followed by more after it.

On the overhead speakers, instead of the urgent and way-too-frequent rapid response and code blue calls, a snippet of Journey's "Don't Stop Believin'" filled the rooms and corridors. Nurses, patient care assistants, unit secretaries, respiratory therapists, physical therapists, occupational therapists, hospitalists, intensivists, and more lined the hallways, and we clapped and sang our hearts out, as much for ourselves as for the patients.

We sang for the ones who did not leave through the front doors but through the basement, hushed and unseen. For all of it, for all of us, we hollered, "Don't stop believin'!" And we believed together.

We are God's instruments of grace and deliverers of mercy against merciless and abominable foes, whether pandemics or traumas, preventable or communicable diseases. Whether ushering these patients through hallways lined with all of us, or to golden streets lined with angels, we don't stop. We won't stop. And we do believe. God is in those rooms and hallways, too, cheering us on. One day there will be no more tears, no more grief, no more disease. Until then, we are God's instruments not just of medicine, but also of peace and joy.

HANDWASHING PRAYER

Thank you, Lord, that whether here or in heaven, tears will someday subside. Thank you that even I get to be your ambassador to these patients.

VITAL SIGNS

Record today's fears, frustrations, and heartbreak:

_____

_____

_____

_____

_____

_____

_____

Record things you are grateful for and where you've seen God working this week:

_____

_____

_____

_____

_____

_____

_____

_____

DAY 28

Then God looked over all he had made,
and he saw that it was very good!
GENESIS 1:31

When I switched from a suburban to an inner-city hospital, I expected many differences in patient population, acuity, and socioeconomic needs. However, few things shocked me as much as when I rounded on room 410 one morning.

Therapy dogs had been a frequent sight at the suburban hospital: gentle Labradors, floppy, friendly Chinese Water Dogs, sweet-as-can-be golden retrievers, all dressed in certified comfort and therapy dog vests with handlers who wore treat-filled aprons. Pediatric and adult patients—and especially staff—looked forward to their visits. Patients sometimes had their own service dogs if they were visually impaired, and in one case, a border collie who could sense an oncoming seizure in his owner and would come into the hall to alert staff.

Room 410 at the inner-city hospital was different. The sign on the door was the first thing to give me pause: "Warning: Therapy Dog."

On this morning at my new job, none of the nurses or aides in report gave any warning or indication for concern about what was behind the door of room 410.

I knocked first—which I always do before entering a patient room—and heard a deep, rolling growl on the other side of the door. I checked my papers in case I'd missed a diagnosis of an airway problem.

"Mr. Collins?" I opened the windowless door a crack.

A deeper, more threatening growl emerged.

"It's okay," a voice called out. "It's just my therapy dog."

Therapy dog. Mmm-hmm.

I walked into the room and eyed a surprisingly small dog on the bed, no official therapy dog vest in sight. The angry beast looked like a cross between a Pomeranian and a Jack Russell, its exceptionally long teeth bared, snarling as it strained against its leash toward me. I wished I'd had some crackers or something that could double as a dog treat in my pocket, though they probably would not have made a difference.

I had to admire the gall of the patient to present it as a therapy dog. Any movement to take the patient's blood pressure, temperature, or take a listen to his chest with my stethoscope was met with further snarls and growls before the dog finally curled itself into a tight comma in the crook of Mr. Collins's arm. Its eyes appeared full of disdain, even slight disgust for me, a stranger, as they followed me around the room.

Later on, concern expressed to my manager was met with a shrug. "You shoulda seen the boxer mix in 508 last week."

BREAKROOM BOOST

Dogs—and pets of all kinds—have a way of making everything better, proven by the groups of golden retrievers who travel from disaster to disaster across the country, by individual dogs who travel to hospitals and nursing homes, by those trained as first responders. It is no wonder patients want their pets with them when they are lonely and sick, no wonder family will defy policies and sneak them to bedsides in backpacks and coolers and jacket lapels. Their tail wags and slobbery, sloppy wet kisses comfort us all.

HANDWASHING PRAYER

Thank you, Lord, for cats and dogs, country walks and birdsong, and even for growling guard dogs—for all your creatures and creation that gives us joy.

VITAL SIGNS

Record today's fears, frustrations, and heartbreak:

_____

_____

_____

_____

Record things you are grateful for and where you've seen God working this week:

_____

_____

_____

_____

DAY 29

I will give you a new heart, and
I will put a new spirit in you.
EZEKIEL 36:26

Posters of Dot Richardson, Jennie Finch, Lisa Fernandez, and other softball players covered the walls of Brittany's room on the pediatric oncology ward. She wore a UCLA Softball T-shirt, and a blue-and-gold fleece blanket featuring softballs and bats covered her legs.

As her oncologist, I had the responsibility of keeping her on track with her treatments. She had only one left, and she didn't want to do it.

No one could blame her for refusing. Bone cancer treatment was brutal, and indeed Brittany had almost died when the last round sent her into septic shock, her blood counts too low from the chemotherapy to fight even the slightest infection, let alone a big one. But the research clearly showed she needed to finish this series of chemotherapy right through to the end.

I sat on the side of Brittany's bed and talked with her and her parents for over an hour about what to expect, how it would help ensure we fought off all the cancer cells—especially the ones we couldn't see in tests—and how we would take extra precautions with immune-boosting medications to help prevent her from getting so sick again.

Brittany wasn't having it.

The more I talked, the more she withdrew, crossing her arms and legs, and refusing to look at any of us.

I studied the gangly teenager in front of me, head bald underneath a pink thick-yarned cap with a fuzzy ball on top. How many special teenage moments had the cruel disease already stolen from her? How could I get through to her now?

Lord, help me find a way to reach Brittany's heart.

My eyes settled on the poster of Lisa Fernandez. I knew about her because my own daughter was a budding women's softball fan and young player. Fernandez was a famed Olympian with three gold medals, and a right-hander out of UCLA, so I risked a guess.

"Fernandez is your favorite?" I asked.

Her eyes flicked in my direction.

"She's pretty amazing."

"What do you know about it?" she snapped.

"Brittany—" her mom started to scold.

I glanced at mom assuringly, then focused on Brittany. "What do you think Lisa might do in your situation?"

Brittany shrugged, continuing to avoid my gaze.

"All the treatments you've had until now, they've been home runs *in* the park. Now we need you to hit one last time, and get the ball *out* of the park. Do you think you can do that?"

She thought about it for several minutes, crossing and uncrossing her arms, her legs. She tugged and adjusted the pink woolly hat.

"Okay," she said, barely audible, and with tears spilling out of her eyes.

Brittany took the treatment like a champ. Not only did she survive, she's now in medical school. I learned that day to never underestimate the power of God—or softball.

BREAKROOM BOOST

Forward feels like the last place we want to go when we are weary and—worse—broken. But like Brittany, sometimes we don't realize how close we are to a record-setting hit if we'll just take one more step, do one more thing for that impossible patient, or encourage that infuriating coworker. It's so often that last big step of faith that makes all the difference.

HANDWASHING PRAYER

Create a clean heart in me, Lord. Help me press on when it's the last thing I want to do for myself or for my patient.

Record today's fears, frustrations, and heartbreak:

_____

_____

_____

_____

EVIDENCE-BASED HOPE

Record things you are grateful for and where you've seen God working
this week:

_____

_____

_____

_____

DAY 30

Then you will experience God's peace,
which exceeds anything we can understand.
PHILIPPIANS 4:7

The distinct reek of black stools matched the murky ambiance of the room as I stepped into the shadows with the night-shift nurse for a bedside report on Loretta. It took me only a few moments to realize this patient had endured a long night of bowel prep, jaunts to the commode, and little to no sleep. Tension hung thick in the air as she managed to smile through gritted teeth and glossy eyes of worry about her impending colonoscopy happening in a mere hour.

The night-shift nurse and I headed back to the hallway with sighs of compassion; for her family history was plagued with extensive amounts of colon cancer, and judging by the tarry residue lingering on the sides of the commode, things were not looking promising. After I finished gathering information on my other patients, I took a deep breath before heading back to Loretta's room for her morning vitals, assessment, and last-minute comfort cares before her procedure.

Our conversation began casually. She shared a bit about her family, her love of baking, and where she was from, yet something in me sensed there was about to be more to the story. Somewhere between the blood pressure cuff and bowel sounds, I was drawn to the discreet nudge within that said, "Sit down," and so I did, alongside the bed. I took her shaky hand and began to listen intently as her internal dam broke loose and she poured her soul out to me about her worries and doubts, believing God had given her more than she could handle. In those sacred moments of just being present with another human, the presence of the Holy Spirit felt abundant in the room, and the lingering heaviness lifted.

She went for her procedure, leaving me alone in her room to change the linens, spray the citrus air freshener, draw back the curtains.

"Lord, please have mercy on this sweet patient. Please give her the strength she needs. Give me the wisdom to be exactly what Loretta needs me to be over the next few hours, no matter the results," I prayed.

The soft rumble of the transport bed coming down the hall sent my heart pounding through my chest, until she was close enough to grab my hand this time, look me in the eye, and blissfully smile, saying, "The doctors can't explain it, but my scan was completely clear." She and I both knew why, and the perfect peace we felt in that moment reminded us both of our ultimate Maker and Healer.

BREAKROOM BOOST

Good news or bad, whether we're giving or receiving it, can toss us like a tiny boat in a raging sea. Without the anchor of faith, the Red Sea was too vast, Goliath too big, Jericho too fortified, the desert too wide, the crowd too large and hungry, and the Cross too much for even Jesus to bear. But in our faithlessness, he is faithful. Always.

HANDWASHING PRAYER

Help me believe, even when others are weak. And help me overcome my own unbelief.

VITAL SIGNS

Record today's fears, frustrations, and heartbreak:

_____

_____

_____

_____

_____

_____

_____

_____

_____

Record things you are grateful for and where you've seen God working this week:

_____

_____

_____

_____

_____

_____

_____

_____

_____

DAY 31

*A person standing alone can be attacked and defeated,
but two can stand back-to-back and conquer. Three are
even better, for a triple-braided cord is not easily broken.*

ECCLESIASTES 4:12

I felt my heart beating in my throat as I walked into the hospital for my fourth day as a first-year internal medicine resident. In the last three days I'd inserted a central line, adjusted too many pressor rates to count, and slept less than ten hours total. I'd be lucky to function today, let alone function well.

The safety net of medical school felt like eons ago as I struggled to catch all the information and assignments for the day, including my own new admission, which felt like trying to work a puzzle without the benefit of the picture on the box.

What if I can't make it in this job? What if my ignorance hurts a patient? What if my fellow residents—or worse, my supervisor—figure out that behind my feigned confidence I feel like a fake? What if I should never have become a physician?

"You're fearfully and wonderfully made." The phrase from Psalm 139 that my mom had said to me every morning as I walked out of the house through grade school, middle school, and high school echoed in my head.

Yeah, right. What if I had missed my true calling of becoming a librarian? Or an investment banker? Or any other profession where I didn't run the risk of actually killing someone?

I will give you strength, I heard the Holy Spirit whisper.

I took a deep breath and found an open computer, where I began pulling up labs and reviewing nursing assessments and vital sign trends. I focused on the pathways and algorithms in my pocket medicine guides.

Beep! Beep! Beep!

The cardiac monitor at the desk screamed, room 633's tracing showing a completely flat line.

I jumped to my feet and ran into the room, leveling the bed, shouting for nursing to grab the code cart.

My hands were positioned above the patient's sternum, and I was about to push down with all my might in the first compression.

"What are you doing, Doc?" the patient said, alarmed.

I looked at his face in confusion, then at the monitor, then back at his face again.

The nurse calmly sauntered into the room and walked past me to shut off the alarms. Then she lifted the patient's gown and replaced a lead that had fallen off his chest.

"Check the patient first." She winked, obviously stifling a chuckle.

I sheepishly returned to my spot at the ICU desk, looking around to see who had seen my ridiculous mistake.

Everyone.

"We're hardest on ourselves," a third-year resident said when he found me later looking hangdog in the locker room. "It's the ones who think they have it all together who probably shouldn't be doctors at all."

A message came across my pager. I was needed back up on the cardiac floor for a genuine emergency. I felt the adrenaline that had called me to medicine begin to return.

I had a lot to learn, but I was in the right place.

BREAKROOM BOOST

We continuously vacillate between feelings of confidence and inadequacy in a profession where education, technology, and processes are constantly changing. Without the guidance, input, and comradery of teammates, none of us would get very far. The mentors, teachers, bosses, and coworkers you encounter over the years are not coincidence. Not all will be favorites, but by God's grace you can learn from them all.

HANDWASHING PRAYER

Lord, show me a coworker I can encourage. And thank you for the people you bring to my life to teach me.

Record today's fears, frustrations, and heartbreak:

_____

_____

_____

_____

EVIDENCE-BASED HOPE

Record things you are grateful for and where you've seen God working this week:

_____

_____

_____

_____

DAY 32

Let's not merely say that we love each other;
let us show the truth by our actions.
1 JOHN 3:18

Cory lay before me on the stretcher in the back of my ambulance. Based on his high-end clothes and shoes and clean-shaven face, I would not have guessed he was struggling with addiction. When I found him, he was nearly dead, but after a few rounds of Narcan he awoke.

On the way to the hospital, he began to share what had led him to where he was today.

"I got caught up with the wrong crowd. I was young," he explained.

He'd held a successful job, and on the outside he seemed to have his life together, but he had been hiding a struggle with addiction for years. He beat himself up the entire way to the hospital, ashamed that he had lost his nearly yearlong sobriety. But he was hopeful that with the support of his girlfriend and family he could stay clean and move beyond this relapse.

One week later, I learned from another team of medics that Cory had overdosed again and died.

When we found Drew in an alleyway the next week, it was too late for Narcan. Still, we tried to resuscitate him. His license showed he was only twenty-one, the same age as me, and I couldn't help but feel as if I were looking in a mirror. We had walked the exact same amount of time on earth, and yet somehow his life had become so much different from mine.

"We need to call it," my partner said, indicating we had done everything we could.

But miraculously, Drew's heart started beating again. The blip of the monitor was the sweetest sound I'd ever heard. Still, I was all but certain he was brain dead, as were the doctors at the hospital, and I felt a sadness I hadn't yet felt in my career. There wasn't time to stick around and see what would happen, so we left for another run.

Later I learned that within a week, Drew walked out of the hospital with zero deficits. I keep in contact with him and check in every few months or so. He's doing well and living a successful life. He is sober.

"I got a second chance," he says.

I meet dozens of Corys and Drews—opposite ends of the opioid crisis spectrum—as do thousands of other paramedics across the country. The opioid epidemic robs people of their lives every day, people who belong to someone, people who are loved by someone. And once in a while, someone recovers.

BREAKROOM BOOST

The stigma and the overwhelming numbers of the opioid epidemic make it difficult not to feel cynical and jaded about these patients. But the relentless cycle of addiction is most painful for the individuals who are addicted, and we often see them in their most hopeless days. The human made in God's image becomes hidden behind the needle scars and desperation. In the limited time we have with them as a caregiver, we can't cure them, but we can show them love.

HANDWASHING PRAYER

Lord, help me not forget there is a human, created in God's image, behind the addict. Help me to love and value each one the way you do.

VITAL SIGNS

Record today's fears, frustrations, and heartbreak:

_____

_____

_____

_____

_____

Record things you are grateful for and where you've seen God working this week:

_____

_____

_____

_____

_____

DAY 33

God has given each of you a gift from his great variety of spiritual gifts.
Use them well to serve one another.

1 PETER 4:10

The yellow leaves of the locust trees framing the emergency department carpeted the ground the day a young mother named Jessie came to us with complaints of chest pain. She had delivered a healthy baby a few days prior, and she thought she had a bad case of heartburn.

The paramedic did an electrocardiogram and presented it to the physician on staff that night.

Everything indicated she was having a heart attack, and as the unit secretary, I knew instantly that every second meant life or death for this young mother. I listened for and activated all of the procedures the team called out, while at the same time typing pager numbers in the phone and orders in the computer. Within minutes, members of the cardiac team arrived, breathless and eager to start their treatments.

I continued to field phone calls and paging responses as the nurses prepared the patient to be transported to the cardiac catheterization lab down the hall. A flurry of staff went briskly from Jessie's bedside to the medication room, to the supply room, and back again. From my spot at the central desk, I could see the look of fear and bewilderment in Jessie's eyes, so I took her a warm blanket.

"You're in good hands, Jessie," I said, tucking the blanket around her legs and chest, careful to leave the various electrodes and other monitor wires in place.

"My husband?" she asked.

"We've called him. He's on his way."

Tears filled her eyes and she reached for my hand. "Thank you."

Team members filled the room again, unlocked the wheels of the gurney, and whisked her off to the cardiac catheterization lab. Half an hour later, we were shocked to hear the advanced life support helicopter landing.

The hospital administrator hurried toward us and confirmed our new mama had an abdominal aortic aneurysm, likely something she'd had for years, and there was nothing they could do to stop it from dissecting at our suburban hospital. She had to be transported immediately to the city hospital, where a team of cardiovascular surgeons were awaiting her arrival.

Jessie was sedated when they wheeled her by my desk to the helicopter, its giant, spinning blades ushering a whirlwind of golden locust leaves into the vestibule, and I found it difficult to focus on any of the other patients that shift, unable to stop thinking about her and her newborn baby, and her husband.

A few hours later, one of the cardiologists who had responded earlier came by the emergency department.

"She's okay," he said, leaning toward me over the top of my workstation. "She had the surgery and is doing well. Thanks to you."

BREAKROOM BOOST

The mundane, administrative parts of our job can seem unimportant until they're needed in an emergency, when the details are often what holds a high-intensity situation together. Bringing a warm blanket, knowing department and pager numbers and protocols by heart, catching and correcting incorrect orders—being faithful with small things makes all the difference in the big things.

HANDWASHING PRAYER

Thank you, Lord, for the gift of team members who work together.

VITAL SIGNS

Record today's fears, frustrations, and heartbreak:

_____

_____

_____

_____

_____

Record things you are grateful for and where you've seen God working
this week:

_____

_____

_____

_____

_____

DAY 34

God is not a God of disorder but of peace.

1 CORINTHIANS 14:33

Mounds of clothes overflowed from our laundry room, evidence that our young-adult children had returned from college for the summer. I'd procrastinated sorting and folding—my least favorite chore—for too long, and now the job appeared insurmountable. I sat on the floor in the center of it and began the vain task of matching socks and stacking piles that would make their way to closets and bedrooms, only to return to this very spot in a week or two.

As I touched each shirt, towel, and pair of pants, I was reminded of the training I'd received from Sandy, a seasoned surgical nurse: Touch the instruments only once.

Timely and accurate setup of surgical instruments and tables is crucial to operating-room function and even the success of surgical procedures. There's a place for everything, and everything needs to be in its place by the time the surgeon enters. The inability to find a clamp or scalpel or suture or sponge when it's needed can result in frustration at the least, and can even put a life at risk.

At first, learning where to put instrument trays and bowls didn't make much sense to me as an operating-room nurse orientee. I felt like sponges should go next to the retractor. The DeBakey forceps seemed too far away and out of place next to the bone saw. Over and over, Sandy came behind my novice attempts and rearranged my ignorant choices, sometimes by seemingly miniscule amounts, that I didn't fully understand until the middle of the surgical procedure, the patient's abdomen covered in blue sterile drapes except for where the abdomen was sliced and stretched wide open, every movement of the surgeon dependent on an intricate plan and accurate instrumentation.

I set another folded T-shirt in my oldest child's clean laundry basket, one item closer to cleaning up the chaos of the laundry room. By the time the last socks were paired, I could see the tile floor again. It was a far cry from the OR, and yet the order was a welcome accomplishment in the chaos of overtime and to-do lists.

"Oooh, my favorite T-shirt," my son said as he whisked in and grabbed the shirt I'd just folded. Then he kissed me on top of my head. "Thanks, Mom."

"You're welcome," I smiled, warmth filling my chest. I realized anew the blessing of having someone to fold laundry for in the first place.

BREAKROOM BOOST

So often the teachings of Christ seem impractical, even inapplicable to the constant chaos and high pressure of the hospital. How can things like overcoming cynicism, refusing to chime in with gossip at the nurses' station, and showing extra care with the most impatient patient really make a difference? Jesus doesn't expect us to turn things around all by ourselves. But holding fast to his teachings ushers in the peace and order he so wants to show the world through us.

HANDWASHING PRAYER

Help me be an instrument of your peace that passes understanding, Lord.

VITAL SIGNS

Record today's fears, frustrations, and heartbreak:

_____

_____

_____

_____

_____

Record things you are grateful for and where you've seen God working this week:

_____

_____

_____

_____

_____

DAY 35

They will walk beside quiet streams and
on smooth paths where they will not stumble.
JEREMIAH 31:9

Bob's wife, Shelley, gave me the "wife look" when they came to my clinic for the first time.

"I hear you're having some knee pain," I said to him.

As Bob's physical therapist, I explained what treatments we could do to help him regain strength and decrease his pain, and he nodded in agreement.

In the opposite chair, Shelley crossed her arms. "Tell her about your hip, Bob."

I looked at Bob, who shifted in his chair. His cheeks reddened, likely from Shelley revealing something he didn't want mentioned.

"I only received a report about your knee. Is there something you'd like to tell me about your hip?"

He opened his mouth to speak, but Shelley beat him to it. "He's been limping since we met in college. He said it was from football, and I've been telling him—"

"She's been telling me for fifteen years to come see a PT," Bob interrupted in a mock told-you-so tone.

"Would you mind walking across the room for me?"

He obliged, and right away I could see what the problem was. But I needed to confirm.

"One more favor. Can you hop up on my table and lie down for a moment?"

He did, and I proceeded to gently manipulate his leg and hip in various directions, until he winced in pain at a couple of moves in particular.

My suspicions confirmed, I stepped back and let him sit up. "Good news. I can fix your knee *and* your hip."

He tilted his head in questioning disbelief. "How's that?"

I explained that I recognized his limp because I'd seen it in other athletes with untreated injuries. "Your limp isn't from the injury; it's from the way you compensated for it. It's basically a bad habit. If you're willing—"

"He's willing," Shelley said.

"I'm willing." He grinned.

With a lot of work, we were eventually able to teach him to walk normally again. He completed therapy and no longer had knee pain, but most of all, he and his wife were excited that he no longer limped!

BREAKROOM BOOST

Sometimes the things that ail us most are only symptoms of a deeper, more insidious affliction. As healthcare workers, we are reluctant to say no to extra shifts, to more projects we don't have time for, to bigger and more acute patient loads. We skip breaks and take on constant change and stick out toxic work situations for too long. Resultant fatigue, depression, and anxiety can spiral into bitterness and a loss of resilience. Carrying this load on our shoulders and limping through the days and months and years, we ultimately lose hope. Reversing the process calls for diligently and persistently pursuing things like healthy boundaries, therapy, wellness programs, and regular intimacy with the Lord. Don't wait until momentary stresses develop into something more chronic. Take care of yourself, so you can take care of others.

HANDWASHING PRAYER

Lord, show me the places in my work life that need better boundaries, and how to take better care of myself with your help, so that I can be a healthy part of the team.

Record today's fears, frustrations, and heartbreak:

_____

_____

_____

_____

EVIDENCE-BASED HOPE
Record things you are grateful for and where you've seen God working
this week:

_____

_____

_____

_____

DAY 36

Not a single sparrow can fall to the ground
without your Father knowing it.
MATTHEW 10:29

The nurse handed me a small white bag that reminded me of the FedEx envelope in which I'd received a soft, bright yellow sweater the day before.

My stomach twisted at the almost imperceptible weight in my hands.

"You ready?" the security officer gently asked, the circle of keys on his belt jingling as he shifted his weight.

"Thank you," the nurse said, then, resigned, turned back to the now-empty room where Lily, born at twenty-three weeks gestation, had lived for four brief days. The door to her room was covered with pink gingham and flower-laden scrapbook pages documenting the brave journey she'd endured, one full of pokes and tubes. The clear plastic incubator now stood empty, next to respirators that were silent and unplugged. The table beside the rocking chair where her mother had sat was stacked high with pink and purple and yellow, sweetly flowered onesies and linen receiving blankets that would never be wrapped around the too-small, translucent-skinned body.

The parents had said their goodbyes, and now it was time for us, the night shift hospital administrator and security officer Carl, to take Lily to the morgue.

Carl's usually jovial, joking facade was unusually silent, as was mine. Irreverent laughter was how we got through tough, emergency-laden nights. But we were silent as we walked down the fluorescent-lit hallways and rode the elevator to the basement of the hospital. White cement-block walls and concrete floors spread before us as we made our way to the small, unmarked door at the end of the hall. It was one thing to deliver the body of an adult there; quite another to deliver a tiny human, cold and impossibly weightless, and lay it on an eight-foot-long metal tray inside an oblong refrigerator.

Nursing school, medical school, and officer training school teach us to harden our hearts, to feign stoicism, to not take our work home with us. But the moments like these are never really forgotten. They just add to the gaping, yawning whys in our hearts—the ones we fall into and grieve at odd moments, like while watching an ocean sunset or misty mountain sunrise; moments that compel us to make our lives matter, and that cause us to constantly question why some never get a chance at all.

BREAKROOM BOOST

Life is short, only a blip in light of eternity. God did not mean for it to be this way. But he will redeem little Lily, and someday bring healing to the broken hearts of all who loved and served her. Holy moments like that are part of our work and our days. Know that. Believe that. Blessed are those who mourn.

HANDWASHING PRAYER

Lord, help me mourn with those who mourn. Thank you that you restore broken hearts.

VITAL SIGNS

Record today's fears, frustrations, and heartbreak:

_____

_____

_____

_____

_____

_____

_____

Record things you are grateful for and where you've seen God working this week:

_____

_____

_____

_____

_____

_____

_____

_____

DAY 37

The Lord isn't really being slow about his promise, as some people think.
No, he is being patient for your sake. He does not want anyone to
be destroyed, but wants everyone to repent.

2 PETER 3:9

Three acute abdomens, one hip fracture, and room 562, a twenty-one-year-old woman going on her fifth week on our unit.

"Can she leave this week?" the charge nurse asked, like a child ten minutes into a long road trip asking, "Are we there yet?"

All of us at the morning multidisciplinary huddle knew the answer.

"One more week," I said, acknowledging their angst. The social worker part of me tried to assuage their frustration. "Her state Medicaid is still pending." And likely would be until after she discharged from the hospital. Brought to our hospital from all the way across the state, she had the classic trifecta of IV drug–addict afflictions: no insurance, osteomyelitis raging in her needle-scarred arm, and IV antibiotics for six weeks without exception.

I'd avoided her room for days, since nothing had changed and I had no good news to offer her. But this morning, guilt convicted me to at least stop in and say hello.

I pushed open the door to her room and found it dark as night, the drapes pulled tight. It was the typical mole-ish existence of most patients in her predicament. The only light was from the glow of the IV pump and the cell phone pressed close to her face.

"Alanna?"

The tightly curled ball of humanity did not move.

I stepped closer. "Hey there, it's Susan, the social worker. Just wanted to check on you, see if you had any questions or concerns?"

A foot wiggled under the covers, and she mumbled something.

"What's that? I can't hear you?"

"Get. Me. Out. of here," she growled, with the addition of several choice expletives.

I felt exasperation and annoyance rising in my chest. I quickly remembered why I had avoided her.

"I'm trying," I offered, doing my best to sound unperturbed and calm. "The Medicaid hasn't come through yet, and the antibiotics have to run their course. Five more days." I focused on the slim crack of light coming from between the thick, blackout hospital drapes. I was frustrated too—with the system, with the lifestyle choices that put her here, with the disease of addiction, with my inability to make a difference for her or to her. I felt the press of moral failure against my heart, something I carried home day after day, no matter how much I tried to laugh it off with my coworkers.

Where was God in this?

BREAKROOM BOOST

Unanswered prayers and unchanging hearts might seem pointless, but sometimes they allow for the time and space a person needs to someday find God. His patience is never-ending, especially for the Alannas of our days. Our perceived lack of success is not a failure—we are another opportunity for God to demonstrate his love to each patient we come into contact with.

HANDWASHING PRAYER

Lord, help me remember every patient I meet is created in your image, and that you don't want anyone to perish.

VITAL SIGNS

Record today's fears, frustrations, and heartbreak:

_____

_____

_____

_____

_____

Record things you are grateful for and where you've seen God working this week:

_____

_____

_____

_____

_____

DAY 38

My soul thirsts for you; my whole body longs for you in this parched and weary land where there is no water.
PSALM 63:1

My colleague had warned me that the family situation of the young patient in room 302 was "challenging," and that the twenty-two-month-old girl with respiratory syncytial virus, RSV, was balancing precariously between the pediatric and critical care units.

Ava had been helicoptered up from a remote part of the state in the middle of the night, and the family would not arrive for hours. Even in their absence, the room reeked of cigarettes.

Well before I reached the side of the crib, I heard Ava's labored breathing, saw her chest rising and falling too fast. I approached the crib as quietly as I could. She slept with her legs tucked under her, curled up like a sweet stink bug, rosebud lips slightly open with a line of drool soaking the sheet, eyelids pale blue and fluttering with dreams.

I hated to disturb her, but her vital signs couldn't wait. Even without a touch or numbers on a monitor, her breathing was obviously too fast and too labored to put them off. As gently as I could, I wrapped the blood pressure cuff around her too-thin arm and tucked the cold end of the thermometer under her arm.

Ava startled and woke, wide-eyed, then pushed herself up to sitting. She rubbed her eyes, her mouth pulling into a pucker. She peeked at me through her toddler hands and spoke an awful curse word I'd only heard come from adults, and even then, only rarely.

Surely I'd misunderstood.

But then she said it three more times, her eyes spilling tears.

Tears pricked my own eyes as I studied the toddler, blonde curls twisted into sweat-soaked tendrils. Now she was standing, her grimy hands gripping the rails and her grimy knees wobbling against the high fever.

"Sweet baby girl," I whispered, bewildered at what kind of world she lived in that her first thought would be to call me a derogatory term I didn't learn until I rode the high school bus. "I'm here to help. I'm only here to help."

She frowned, wary of my offer of the sippy cup of Pedialyte I'd tucked in with her sheets and bath supplies. But eventually she grabbed it and pulled great gulps from it, straining to swallow faster than the lid allowed.

I filled the bath pan with warm water and baby soap and brought it to the crib. She drank and drank, eyeing me with suspicion as I worked the grime from her feet, her knees, her elbows and tiny fingers until all of her shone damp and pink.

I wondered how long it had been since she'd felt so clean.

BREAKROOM BOOST

Just when we think we've seen and heard the worst of everything, we are faced with an even more unimaginable, heartbreaking situation. The brokenness is never-ending. But every hungry mouth we feed, every thirst we quench, every battered body we salve and clothe, every act of love to a stranger is serving an eternal purpose. Even if we can't see it in the moment, Jesus promises it matters. Especially to him.

HANDWASHING PRAYER

Lord, renew my compassion for those who live in unbearable situations. Help me remember that in caring for others, I am caring for you.

VITAL SIGNS

Record today's fears, frustrations, and heartbreak:

_____

_____

_____

_____

_____

EVIDENCE-BASED HOPE

Record things you are grateful for and where you've seen God working this week:

_____

_____

_____

_____

_____

DAY 39

They all ate as much as they wanted,
and afterward, the disciples picked up
twelve baskets of leftovers.

MATTHEW 14:20

I counted the patients, and I counted the nurses again.

Were the printouts wrong? Or my calculations?

Neither.

We were short-staffed.

Again.

I called the hospital administrator. "We need three more nurses."

The long sigh on the other end of the line told me all I needed to know. The hospital had been doing everything to try to bring in more staff: time-and-a-half pay, double pay, and yet the staffing ratios didn't budge.

Two nurses were on maternity leave and two more were on family leave. My manager was having a hard time justifying travel-nurse and resource-nurse pay. No one wanted to float to our adult medical unit, the one full of heavy-assist, complicated old people, the one the rest of the hospital referred to as "the armpit of the hospital."

"Lord, can't you multiply nurses like you multiplied loaves and fishes?" I waited in vain for him to answer, simultaneously praying the ringing phone the secretary picked up was not a day-shift nurse calling off work.

I pulled another blank piece of paper from the copy machine and began to graph out yet another staffing scenario, this time without the three nurses we so desperately needed. I would have to stay late.

I started a text message to my husband: *Can you get the kids on the bus? Have to cover until I can find more nurses.*

He couldn't—his own boss was becoming frustrated by his frequent late arrivals, caused by weeks of short staffing.

The unit secretary swiveled her chair around, her face deadpan.

"No—don't tell me—"

Her face broke into a wide smile. "We got two resource nurses."

It wasn't the three I'd hoped for, but it could work.

It was loaves and fishes.

I erased the text to my husband.

"Thank you, Lord," I prayed, out loud. "Thank you, thank you, thank you."

BREAKROOM BOOST

From providing for the Israelites for forty years in the desert (their shoes didn't even wear out!), to turning water to wine for a wedding party, to weeping with sisters begging for the life of their brother, Lazarus, God hears and tends to all prayers. He is big enough to be sovereign over worldly matters, and big enough to be with us in every moment of our day too . . . even staffing crunches, even cars that break down, even if all we can say to him is, "Help."

HANDWASHING PRAYER

Sometimes all I can pray is, "Help me, Lord." I'm so grateful that is enough for you.

VITAL SIGNS

Record today's fears, frustrations, and heartbreak:

_____

_____

_____

_____

_____

_____

_____

Record things you are grateful for and where you've seen God working this week:

_____

_____

_____

_____

_____

_____

_____

DAY 40

Cry aloud before the Lord. . . .
Let your tears flow like a river day and night.
LAMENTATIONS 2:18

Screams pierced the quiet of the dark, early-morning halls of the surgical unit, two wards away from where I'd been visiting with night-shift staff at the nurses' station. Those of us able to leave our stations for an emergency ran toward the shrill cries, and as we approached, we were stopped by the unit's charge nurse.

"It's okay," she said in a hushed voice, hands indicating we could settle our adrenaline-charged concern. "Room 430 passed. The family—they're having a hard time."

I was a new graduate, and my religious and cultural upbringing had never allowed me the opportunity to witness the way some people so freely emote their pain.

My instincts wanted to shush this loud, expressive extended-family group, to redirect them, to push a box of tissues into their grief-curled fists. I was reminded of my psychology professor's admonition that doing so was equivalent to telling a patient to hush.

Against the wall outside the room, three young stair-step children sat, wide-eyed and watching as their parents, aunts, and uncles paraded their broken hearts up and down the hall on full display. I knelt down beside the kids.

"You guys okay?"

The oldest one nodded.

"Papa died," the youngest one said.

"I'm sorry."

"I love Papa," said the middle son.

Initial apprehension and dislike toward what I perceived as a ridiculous display of emotion peeled off and left me raw with emotion for these little ones.

I imagined the three of them climbing across their grandfather's lap at Sunday lunches, vying for his attention. I imagined them without the man who, like most grandparents, was someone who offered deep and joyful exclamations of adoration over his grandchildren. I looked at their mother, wailing for her father; their grandmother, wrapped in the arms of one of her sons, their uncle. I couldn't imagine the giant void they now had to face going forward, and I felt ashamed for judging their loud grief. I might not understand it, but I recognized that they needed to express what was in their hearts that day, the best way they knew how. And I needed to give that my utmost respect.

BREAKROOM BOOST

The ways in which people feel and show emotion are as varied as the number of people God created. He welcomes the tears and cries of mourners, for they are blessed. And he welcomes the struggle of caring hearts like ours who search for the right way to respond.

HANDWASHING PRAYER

Lord, help me give love and grace to the grieving and to those I do not understand.

VITAL SIGNS

Record today's fears, frustrations, and heartbreak:

_____

_____

_____

_____

_____

_____

_____

_____

Record things you are grateful for and where you've seen God working
this week:

_____

_____

_____

_____

_____

_____

_____

_____

_____

ACKNOWLEDGMENTS

No one practices medicine at any level without a team. During my twenty-five-plus years of nursing, I have been blessed to work alongside the best teammates of all time. Among them are APNs, RNs, LPNs, nursing aides, physicians, rehabilitation therapists, security officers, and everything in between. Some of them were kind enough to contribute to this book, and I cannot thank them enough: Jane Pond Barrett, pharmacist; Sara Bretsch-Klingkammer, RN; Daphne Bryant, MSN, RN, CFRN, CEN; Meredith Brooks, NRP; Carol Lee Cherry, BSN, MSN, CNE, RN (and my favorite nursing professor!); Tracy Davis, BSN, RN, CCRN; Ann DeCarlo, BSN, RN; Lana Greene, RN, BS; Avery Heatwole, BSN, RN; Robert Herren, Deputy Police Chief; Marty Hoyt, RN; Ruth Kain, MSN, RN, NE-BC; Amanda Kutoloski, MSPT; Kelli Mueller, BSN, RN; Candy Roberts; Sarah Rohr, MSN, RN, FNP-C; Laquinta Salary, BSN, RN; Kim Sparkman-Berger; Alyce Swisher, BSN, RN; Douglas N. Tannas, MD; Crysta Wilson, BSN, RN; Eric Yancy, MD, pediatrician.

For the countless other colleagues who are not listed here by name, please know that I would not be the nurse—or person—I am without every single one of you.

To my colleagues on the Tyndale House Publishers team, thank you for your wisdom, exceptional editing, and kind grace, and for fast-tracking this to get it into the hands of healthcare heroes who need hope now more than ever. To Don Pape, for being my undeserved cheerleader and hero in his own right. And to Sarah Freese and Greg Johnson, for your constant support and encouragement as agents and friends.

To my family: my husband, Scott, for constantly referring to me as "writer," even when I felt as far from that as ever. To all my sons, for encouraging me to chase my dreams, even as I have encouraged you to chase yours, including my son and legacy healthcare hero Tucker, BSN, RN. In memory of my grandmother, Mary Jane Kossack, a highly respected nurse who graduated from the St. Joseph South Bend School of Nursing in 1940, for the inspiration she continues to provide me. And to Ann L. Hendrich, PhD, RN, for giving the girl in the pink suit a chance all those years ago.

Finally and above all, to my Lord and Savior Jesus Christ, who guides my heart and my pen, and continues to use my brokenness for good and for hope in spite of me.

Amy K. Sorrells is a longtime believer in the power of story to change lives. Her diverse writing career includes more than two decades of freelance writing, including medical journal publications and a popular op-ed newspaper column.

The driving mission behind all her writing is to bring words of hope to a hurting world. Praised by reviewers for the way they both poetically and accurately portray real-life hardship and hope, Amy's novels are inspired by social issues that break her heart and the Bible stories that reflect God's response to those issues. Her first novel, *How Sweet the Sound*, was a response to her personal questions about how God redeems the pain of sexual abuse. *How Sweet the Sound* won the 2011 Women of Faith Writing Contest.

Since then, she has published three more novels, *Then Sings My Soul*, *Lead Me Home*, and *Before I Saw You*. Amy's novels have been short-listed for various fiction awards. She also designed and edited a photographic devotional journal called *Morning by Morning*.

In addition to being a writer, Amy is also grateful to be a veteran nurse in a variety of positions for over twenty-five years, her favorite of which have been at the patient bedside. In her spare time, she enjoys DIY and woodworking projects, and loves doting on her husband, three young-adult sons, and their three retrievers at their home in central Indiana.